HELLO FUTURE

GOODBYE PAST

IVAN ROSE

I.S.B.N. 978-0-9523667-0-6

Please contact me for more information at ivanrosetherapy@gmail.com

Important message

Hypnotherapy downloads have been explicitly created for this book and are an essential part of this self-help learning program.

To receive your FREE hypnosis audio downloads please register at

https://ivanrose.co.uk/reg

I

I was born worthy and I am deserved of a fulfilled and happy life

I allow universal energy of spirit and mind to facilitate through me

I promote kindness and love towards others as well as myself

I reject the forces of negativity and embrace positivity in all I do

I forgive others as I forgive myself, so that I can be at peace

I am not better than anyone else and no one is better than me

I reciprocate respect to all without discrimination

Yours Truly

Seeds, they randomly scatter across the lands

The process of nature working at what it understands

The universe gets to work, from the seeds that are sown

Some grow in bunches, and some grow alone

Some blossom early, while others have to wait

Everything has its own time, regardless of it's date

Flowers need assistance, from the sun and the rain

And some of us need help to ease hardship and pain

But thrive, yes you will, if you open your mind

New learning, guidance, and happiness, are what you will find

Whatever your situation, it's not a matter of fate

To reinvent, to change your thoughts, it's never ever too late

CONTENTS

Introduction

No one needs to live a life burdened with anxiety, fear or stress-related mental health issues, and positive change is available to anyone who wants it enough. It is merely new knowledge, learning and practice. With the exception of psychosis related mental illness, there are three areas of our mind that, when in great shape, will give us excellent mental health. When we learn and implement the rules and practices of the three tiers of mental wellbeing, we develop the ability and the power to change our mental health state, and the more you work at it, the more it improves.

You can transform your mental health state with new learnings, practices, and hypnosis audios, expertly crafted for those struggling with insecurity, anxiety, fear, frustration, low moods, low self-esteem, lack of confidence, poor self-control, or continual feelings of stress.

Learn the rules of the **Three Tiers of Mental Wellbeing** to overhaul your mental health.

1. Management and control of your self-talk/inner dialogue.

2. Emotional closure of subconsciously stored distressing memories from past events.

3. The development of self-value, self-acceptance, and self-trust.

Life is a physical and spiritual journey of experience, discovery, and learning. When we are first born, we cannot take care of ourselves and are entirely dependent on our parents or caregivers. Neither do we have any control over our environment, ethnicity, or our physical and mental attributes. However, as we mature, we develop the ability to dictate the direction of our lives, make choices, and control our state of happiness and levels of success. Millions of people worldwide feel that they have been born into the wrong families or that their childhood was not what it should have been. Whatever your childhood circumstances, you can do little about it until you become old enough for independence. It is essential to know that yours and everyone's life is purposeful. We all have a reason for being here because we all play a part in others' lives. Every brick in a supporting wall is equally as important.

Everyone experiences difficulties and challenges throughout their lives. Each person's perception is unique because we all interoperate our experiences in different ways. None of us know when our life will end, but when it does, how do you want to be remembered? When you die, your legacy will be all that is left.

Your reputation and life actions affect others' wellbeing, family members, friends, offspring, and potentially many generations after you, so how you are remembered does matter.

During our living experience, we have a duty of care towards ourselves, and those we influence.

Regardless of your circumstances or upbringing, a happy, prosperous, and balanced life is available to you. You can orchestrate the life experience you desire by managing your mental state. Stability of mind is critical for our general wellbeing and happiness. To achieve this we must learn how to acquire optimal control over our coping abilities, cognitive thinking, behaviors, and manage our emotions.

We cannot expect things to change if we do not make a positive change or know how to change, and so if we want a better next chapter of our life, then we have to start working on it in the now. When we are unhappy but doing nothing about it, we are maintaining our sad state. There is no limit to how many times we can change, and so we can keep changing until we get it right.

Top tip; If we relate our life to a book, and viewed our life story as an evolving development of different chapters, we give ourselves hope. When we endure challenging times or when things are not working out, remember that it's only a moment in time, and know that it will pass. When we are experiencing difficult times, this is the best time to implement change, ready for a better next chapter.

Think of yourself as a work of art that you keep refining and shaping until you become what you want to be. *It doesn't matter where you've been, only where you're going.*

Chapter 1

Change is Possible for Everyone

Have you ever wondered why some people seem to be more fortunate, prosperous, better balanced, and generally happier than others?

The main reason for this comes down to childhood circumstances, experiences, and learnings. Parents or caregivers with excellent parenting skills give a child the time, love, nurturing, teachings, guidance, and support they need, laying the foundation for a happy and stable adulthood. If we learn wrong, we act, behave, and think wrong. Still, if we have not had the good fortune of a nurtured upbringing, it doesn't mean that we cannot acquire it. We can learn and develop at any age. We can achieve balance, inner happiness, and all the successes we desire. Once we have become adults, then we are mature students, and we are likely to have become streetwise in the process of a non-nurtured childhood. This means those mature students are streetwise, unlike those that have led sheltered lives. This provides adult students with an advantage when reshaping their future. We can change the way we think, feel, and behave with new learning and practice. By improving our mental health, we can control our feelings, thoughts, and actions. It can enable us to manifest incredible things, including material and financial abundance, meaningful relationships, and inner peace. With the right learning and attitude, we can pursue and achieve anything we want. There is no age or time restriction, and it doesn't rely on money or any unique talents. All we need is to be willing, open-minded, and prepared to work at it.

Know something fundamental. Whatever your childhood circumstances or the relationship you have had or not had with your birth parents, they gave you something exceptional. They gave you life, the most incredible gift any person can receive. Perhaps you are someone that feels aggrieved, having missed out on a nurtured upbringing, come from a broken home, or maybe adopted. If so, remember, whatever troubles you have experienced, that you have a beating heart and the ability to create change. Unless you have a disability, you can equally enjoy all the pleasures of physical experience; to see, taste, smell, touch, hear and feel, and the mental stimulation that brings. You also have an unwritten future, which means you have an unlimited opportunity. Your past does not have to dictate your future, and you do not need to accept your present circumstances as the cards you were dealt with. Your past history should serve as a foundation, not as a punishment, and you can start the ball rolling for change right this second if you choose. You are just one decision away.

No manual comes with childbirth. Our parents or caregivers rely on what they learned from their parents or caregivers and their experiences. From birth, we learn in a sequence of layers. Only once we have mastered one particular skill can we then determine the next, sit, crawl, walk, run, etc. Unfortunately, many parents or caregivers fail to teach or equip their children with the tools they need for the best chance of a fulfilled and balanced life as an adult through no fault of their own. Being overly spoilt, overly strict, or too relaxed will not help children become stable adults. Neither will abandonment, lack of attention, broken home, volatile or argumentative environments, poverty, mistreatment, lack of love or empathy, wrongful teachings, immoral or dishonest role models. Growing up in these conditions is likely to cause instability. And this can lead to dysfunctional behavior or anxiety-related issues such as insecurity, low confidence, low moods, nervousness, over-analyzing, worrying or thinking, frustration, anger, obsessive-compulsive disorder, and general fear.

For many, it can develop into depression, habits, addiction, aggression, and even criminal activity.

Whatever country, family, class, or environmental circumstances you were born into, every person on the planet experiences difficulty and unavoidable loss, and there are no exceptions. Many believe that our path is chosen before birth for the learning experiences we need in our lifetime to evolve spiritually. Whatever your personal belief is, you have to work with the tools you have and accept the life experience you have been given. Going against it will only make it more difficult. Whatever the goal for your journey on earth is, you must try to make it as enjoyable and as comfortable as possible.

It's hard growing up as an underdog, not feeling loved, and feeling alone. Fortunately, we are only children for a short period of our lives and, at 18 years old, are considered adults, which means that we start a new life at 18 years old, that of an adult. Every year after that age is another year of self-learning and another year further away from childhood. When you become 36 years old, you have lived your upbringing years all over again. Yet many well past that age continue to blame their situation and life circumstances on their upbringing. We can choose to blame everything that goes wrong on the past, or we can use our past to make things right, turning a disadvantage into an advantage, not an excuse for when things do not work out. And this is why it's crucial for those who have had challenging upbringings to let the past go.

The past has gone, and it's in the past for a reason, so leave it there.

We are born survivors, and we come from a long line of survivors. Millions of people before you that were not strong enough to survive died. You come from sturdy stock, which means that you are genetically strong, and it's important to recognize this. You may feel that others are stronger minded than you, but that may not be accurate. Our strength of mind is a learned power. Think about all the difficulties in your past that you have already overcome. I'm not saying that it has been easy, or pleasant but the fact is that you have overcome them, regardless of how tough or challenging it has been. Mental toughness has no limit; it's a mind-set. The ability to overcome obstacles and past difficulties is an attitude of determination accompanied by knowledge. Being strong-minded is not about toughness, or being aggressive, or mean. It's about managing your thoughts and feelings, controlling your actions, recovering from difficulties, and going forward with courage, conviction, and self-belief.

The best things in life are free, and I'm not talking about the toy in a Happy Meal. I'm talking about the beauty of nature, our physical and mental health, faith, love, family, friends, happiness, and the air we breathe. Among many other things, these bring us immense pleasures and are not only free; they are priceless. No amount of money can buy these things - they are irreplaceable.

We cannot blame ourselves for our childhood experiences, as we relied on our influencers' teachings. If we were not well taught or had poor role models, we would have grown up with false beliefs as we adapt to our environment and circumstances.

Each one of us will behave and react according to our surroundings. Anyone hungry or desperate enough would steal, lie, and cheat if they had to. Desperation can cause anyone to do anything. Our survival instincts will always do their best to protect us and will motivate to do whatever is needed to survive.

With good role models, we become confident and assured. We learn how to behave appropriately and take responsibility for the consequences of our actions. Whatever you have been through in the past makes no difference to what you can become. People reinvent themselves all the time, and you can reinvent yourself. Each of us has a talent within us, but you cannot become exceptional if you do not develop those talents. With newly learned behavior and thinking patterns, you can see things differently. When you see things differently, you act and respond differently, and that is life-changing.

Your subconscious mind seeks out the help, guidance, and learning it needs to create the changes you need to improve your life quality. All it takes to start the transformation journey is desire, curiosity, and to be open-minded and optimistic about the possibilities available to you.

Bliss must come from within, not from others.

Chapter 2

How I Rose to this Destiny

As a child growing up in the late 60s and 70s, I was the unfortunate kid that most would have predicted to become one of life's losers. I was short, skinny, buck teethed, one sighted, wimpy, and suffered from asthma, plus I was shy. Bullies could sense me a mile away because I stood out like a redneck at the opera wearing a wife-beater vest. And then there was my name, Ivan Rose. Even I wondered if I was Russian, and it brought me a lot of unwanted attention as a child. Other kids would call me pansy or weed, which did not help my nervous disposition. My Mother was rigorous, my father absent, and my two younger brothers, unlike me, were very boisterous, and I was scared of everything. I suppose I should be grateful that I didn't have a hunch on my back as it would have made my paper round hell, - it was very hilly where I lived.

I remember being around seven years old and invited to a friend's house to play across the street. After being there for just a few minutes, I had a surreal experience. I felt the calmness, warmth, and love of their family unit, which profoundly affected me. From that moment, I knew.

After that incident, I believed that I had been born into the wrong family. Surely this must be a mistake, I would think. I used to daydream massively and was ridiculed for this, only to learn as an adult that having an incredible imagination is a gift and a blessing- it's called creativity. It was mostly an outdoor life, and my brothers and I would always be out on the streets playing and getting into mischief.

I would often venture off for miles on a bicycle with a friend. I remember the first time I did this and was around nine years old. After coming out of an extended cut way, I thought I had found another country. Compared to where I came from it was upmarket, and I was going to move there as soon as I was old enough.

I would play a lot of soccer when I wasn't falling off my bike. Still, I think it is fair to say that I wasn't a natural soccer player; I was about as useful on the soccer pitch as a tanning salon on a Caribbean beach. I was always the last to be chosen when dividing up for teams. My childhood was never dull as there was regularly some drama going on. It could be indoors, outdoors, and often, involved neighbors. It was shall we say, a very eventful project neighborhood, and I survived.

It was the third day at my new high school. Every morning I would make a cup of tea and take it up to my Mother in bed. One particular morning I knocked and entered the bedroom to find she had a new partner with her. I hadn't met him before, and he commented on my school tie; recognizing the school, he asked me if I knew his 12 years old son Steven. I was utterly shocked because it so happened that he was my new best friend who sat next to me in class. I couldn't wait to tell Steven what had happened, and off I went to school and told him the story. Initially, this made our friendship more robust, and we would hang out together outside of school, and I stayed at his house overnight on several occasions. Things started to change when we were messing around one night, and he kicked me full-on in the face, pretending that it was an accident.

A few months later, he and another classmate had work experience in a factory close to the town center on each Tuesday evening. Steven's friend was also called Stephen, and he told me that they could fix it for me to work there. I was excited, and so we arranged to meet outside the factory gates at the end of their shift the following week for me to meet the boss.

It was a cold and dark evening, and I had caught the bus into town to meet them. I waited at the gates, expecting to go in with them for an interview. They told me that the person I needed to speak with was not there, so we walked back towards the town center and under the subway to the bus station. My hands were in my pockets at the time when suddenly, Stephen screamed something derogatory at me and punched me straight in the face. Then the other Steven joined in and knocked me to the ground. They started kicking me in the face, head, and body for several minutes, both wearing steel toe-capped safety boots. It felt like hours, but I somehow managed to drag myself up. I was profusely bleeding and staggered off. As they saw me leaving, they started to come back for me again, and I am not sure how I found the energy, but I ran like an Olympic athlete on amphetamine. The roadrunner wouldn't have caught me that night; I was petrified. The experience left me in an awful state and took several weeks to heal. Still, the experience traumatized me and affected my mental health for several years after.

Around the same time I learned that my Mother's partner, Steven's father, was a violent drunk. Over the next four years or so, I frequently witnessed episodes of alcohol-fuelled violence. I lived with fear and saw many fights; the house smashed up, and more drama than a London theatre. One particular night, after the pubs had kicked out, I was awoken, dragged out of bed, and marched downstairs to find my Mother and brothers stood in line. It was around midnight, and my Mother was bleeding. I stood there in shock, wearing only my underwear. We were all being verbally abused and threatened, so I decided to make a run for it. I dashed to the door and ran out onto the streets. There was snow on the ground, and I didn't know what to do, and so I ran to another street where I saw a house with a light on.

Knocking on the door, the owner called out, "who is it" to which I replied, "it's me; I need help" An older couple opened the door and invited me in. They seemed shocked. I guess if I responded to my front door knocking at 12.15 am in the winter to a 13-year-old boy wearing just his underwear, I would be too. Unsure what to do, they invited me in and called the police. My feet were throbbing, and I was shivering, and they gave me a blanket. The police officers arrived quickly, and the officer gave me his coat and took me home. Refusing to stay at home, I told the officer that I would go to a friend's house, to which they agreed. There were no domestic violence laws in those days, so I grabbed some clothing and was dropped off by the police officers at a local shopping area. I did not have a friend to go to as I lied to get away from the house. After a few hours in an alleyway, I went back home, sneaking into the shed at the bottom of the garden where I shivered until the morning.

The next day I decided to get my own back, and so I opened the trunk of my Mother's partner's car and took his toolbox; he was a plumber and had some heavy tools. It was a struggle, but I dragged them down to the block of apartments at the bottom of the road, placing them by the trash. I should have thrown them in the garbage, but I didn't. I left them in sight, hoping someone would steal them. I mean, it was the sort of place where if someone found a dead body, they would search them first for valuables and cash before calling the police. Turned out that a local person found the toolbox, and somehow they were returned. And I, of course, denied everything. I started playing truant from school at 13 years old, and became a runaway teenager. I would throw a bag out of my bedroom window, pretend to go to school, and I would be gone. I had usually slept in a tent throughout my running away but also in derelict houses, lorry cabs, telephone kiosks, and empty garages or sheds.

On one occasion, a friend and I ran away from home and decided to track his father down that he hadn't seen in 5 years. He believed that his father was in St Ives in Cornwall, UK, around 300 miles from my home-town. We were caught jumping a train without tickets by the police and found out we were runaways. We were put into a children's home for the night until his parents came down and collected us. I was grounded for the whole of the six weeks school holiday in my bedroom. I had several times refused to go home, and as a result, spent a couple of short spells in children's homes.

Things were not pleasant at home. I did not like being in a house that could turn into chaos at any time. We often hear parents threatening to call welfare to get their children to behave better; Well, I contacted them, I would leave school and make my way to the welfare offices and ask them to help me as I refused to go home.

A few years later, I applied to join the Royal Navy before leaving school. Sadly, I failed the medical due to my eyesight, but leaving home was a must for me, so as soon as I left school, two months before my 16th birthday, I had left home. I had no fixed abode and relied on friends for somewhere to stay. I also spent many nights homeless, sleeping on the streets, or anywhere I could. Unfortunately, I found myself hanging out with some unsavory characters due to my circumstances, which caused me a lot of hardship. Still, I learned some pretty sharp street skills in the process. Every negative brings a positive.

Talk about naive, I had just reached 16 years old, and through an Uncle, I was offered a job cleaning in a hotel. On my first day, while cleaning the toilet areas, I noticed a red blob of a jelly-like substance on the floor, which I was a little wary of, so I didn't clean it up; in fact, I wouldn't go near it. Every day it grew bigger and bigger, and I became increasingly concerned about it. After avoiding it for a period of time, I was reprimanded for not cleaning the floors. I explained that I didn't know what the substance was, and that was why I left it alone, only to finally find out in the end that it was red liquid soap dripping onto the floor from the holder. I really thought that it was some type of insect nest or something to do with aliens.

In my early twenties, I found employment as a painter. It was by accident when an acquaintance that had won all of my money in a card game felt sorry for me, well not that sorry for me, I'm sure. He said he could help me get a job painting even though I wasn't experienced, probably so I would have more money to lose to him next time. The following day and on his instruction, I called the company he worked for and managed to talk my way into a job.

Off I went to start my life as a painter; believing my newfound friend was going to help me was my first mistake because, upon arrival, he was nowhere in sight. He was apparently on another job. More like taking the week off with the money he won from me -he was a shady character. A few days later, I decided to see him, only to learn that he had moved out a week earlier, and the other tenants had no idea where he had gone.

I was working now as a painter. I took instruction from a lovely chap called Jim. He was the foreman, and as I soon became aware, a fully committed Jehovah's Witness. For some reason, he took a bit of a shine to me, as he gifted me an energy bar on the first tea break, which left me praying on the pot for three days due to severe constipation. I listened to religious tapes, and lectures, every break-time; guess it was a small price to pay to hold my job. However, when asked to go door knocking at weekends, I drew the line, explaining that I had a phobia of dogs caused by an earlier paper round experience. I was then encouraged to attend church on Sundays but managed to dodge that one – thank God. A short while later, I was subsequently made redundant, which, let's face it, is another way of saying, you're fired.

After a whole six weeks of inspired training and a full complement of paintbrushes in my trunk, I considered myself a professional; I was now a time served painter. I even thought about changing my name to I-van Goff! There I was armed with my new bible, a local business directory, and hey presto. I had my own painting company. I would cold call businesses offering free quotations to find work. It worked well except that I was terrified of heights and spent most of my time up a ladder or on a scaffold tower, which was enduring. My buddy, who I worked with, happened to have a hip problem and could not climb ladders, telling me that his hip required surgery, so I had to do all of the high work. My legs used to shake every morning like an alcoholic suffering Parkinson's in a rehab facility. I prayed daily not to fall; it was my morning ritual. I eventually learned that the reason my buddy was unable to do any ladder work had nothing to do with requiring surgery. It was because he had been wearing his pants too tight.

Things eventually started to improve financially, but it didn't last long as the recession in the mid-80s arrived. Plus, I had an accident falling into an old concrete coal bunker when the lid moved. As I fell, I remember thinking that I was going to break my leg. I stretched my arm out to stabilize myself with a paint scraper in my hand. Before realizing what was going on, I had inadvertently punched through the 6mm plate glass window, fell into the coalbunker, and lacerated my arm, severing a nerve and two tendons. It wasn't a good situation and required emergency surgery. I had to walk around with my arm set in plaster and my wrist cocked at 45 degrees for eight weeks. I looked like I was carrying a swan. Looking back, I missed an opportunity; I should have tried my hand at ventriloquism; I mean, I tried everything else.

From a very young age, I had been trying to make a buck; you name it; I had tried it, car cleaning, carol singing, door-to-door sales, even begging. On one particular occasion,

I started a cooker cleaning service business, which ended abruptly. It ended on the first day and was my first and last cooker cleaning job. I had mistakenly bought the wrong chemicals, although I believe that the Muppet in the hardware store sold me the wrong ones. I had used them on a customer's four-week-old cooker. The cleaning chemicals were a little too overpowering. It was unfortunate that the chemicals burned off all the markings for the control settings. I often wonder how she got on because it must have been tricky to use the stove after that. Maybe she bought a new one or redrew them with a felt tip pen. It was the look on her face that I remember when I said, "there you go, all nice and clean for you now," to which she replied, "Oh yeah – that's clean, that's way to clean for me; I mean, how can I read the knobs? I can't tell the oven from the grill. Her eyes were bulging like a constipated frog.

One time I accidentally spilled wood stain all over a fellow painter's head while working above him. He had what was called a wedge cut, a hairstyle worn longer on one side, and very fashionable at the time. Chris was a cocky guy, and his hair was his pride and joy. With his denim dungarees and plastic sandals, he thought he was God's gift to women. It was an oil-based wood stain, natural mahogany in color. I remember my overly full paint pot becoming stuck between my leg and the ladder as I tried to change position. As I grappled with it, a large blob dripped from the pot's side and landed perfectly onto the center of his head. It felt like it was happening in slow motion. I remember that cringing feeling as it floated toward him. It was a bullseye shot. At that point, I was grimacing like a 300lb man trying to pass a kidney stone while stuck in a toilet cubicle. A small amount of wood stain travels a long way for anyone who doesn't know. In his panic, he frantically tried to rub it off with his hands. He looked like a dancing Elf being attacked by a bunch of wasps. And in doing, he had spread it right throughout his hair.

We made attempts to wash out the stain, which included power washing his head with freezing water in the middle of a construction site on a cold day. We knocked on a resident's door explaining what had happened, and she let us in to use her bathroom, using every cosmetic product she had in her cabinet, including her child's bubble bath – it was a pretty intense time, especially for Chris. Nothing was working.

After a few hours of unsuccessful mayhem, I suggested we drove into town to find a hairdresser, only to see them all closed, as it was Good Friday. He became more and more demoralized by the second. He eventually conceded defeat, his mouth drooping like a pregnant goats belly. It seemed like the end of the world for Chris, so he suggested I took him to the nearest bar to drown his sorrows. We began chatting with some locals inside the bar, and Chris explained to them what had happened. I went to the bathroom, and as I returned, I noticed his hair had started to dry out. He looked like he was wearing a pound of dried spaghetti on his head. I felt terrible about what had occurred, but so hilarious. I laughed all weekend with uncontrollable laughter whenever I tried to explain to anyone what had happened to my work colleague.

The following Tuesday, I returned to work and barely recognized him; his hair was all gone, shaved off, and he was not a happy bunny. He looked so different; in fact, the other lads nicknamed him killer. Glaring at me, he insisted that I pay for the overalls that he said I had ruined. Feeling guilty, I spent the money, and after that, he hardly ever spoke to me again, and when the job ended, we lost contact.

Later that year and needing to find some inside work due to the weather, I signed up for a wall texturing course. After completing the 5-day training period, I was ready to go, so I placed an advert in the local free paper. I received a phone call asking me to texture a lounge ceiling and also to erect coving. However, I had never put coving up before and had no idea how to cut the miters for the corners. It didn't go well, and I ended up with lots of smaller pieces scattered over the floor. When finished, it looked like a patchwork quilt. I tried my best to reassure the owner that it would look beautiful when painted and that she could "fill the gaps." Refusing to pay me, I said jokingly, "If you don't pay me, I will just have to take it down," to which she replied, "Yes please," and slammed the door in my face.

In the late 1990s, the UK government passed a law requiring all electrical appliances to have plugs pre-fitted. I was rather pleased having experienced several electric shocks previously by ad hocking wires. Around that time, I figured out that perhaps I wasn't made for manual or DIY orientated work. So I started to think about other types of ways of making a living. During this time, I learned to play some guitar chords, wrote some songs, and formed a few friends' garden shed band. We had fun, and I was also the singer; well, maybe I shouldn't boast that I was the singer because my voice scared people, including me. The other band members were all much more talented than I was and told me that although they liked the songs I wrote, someone else should sing them and that I should concentrate on writing. Emotionally wounded over this and taking it personally, I retreated to my cave and quit, deciding to do something that I could do alone.

My next idea came, and another project was born. It was to write a book, which I handwrote called The Run. Writing was something that I was always OK at. I wanted to prove that I could actually achieve something on my own and without help. When I completed the book, it felt so rewarding to do something on this scale. I mean, it wasn't a piece of literary genius or anything, but it was mine, and I had 500 copies printed. I had little chance of doing well without any marketing ability or money to spend, but that was OK, as I didn't write the book to make money. I did it for the satisfaction of self-achievement.

Some books I gave away, and a bunch I put into a local bookstore. Sadly and just my luck at the time, shortly after taking my book in-store, the store went bankrupt, through no fault of mine, by the way. It ended that I lost those books and donated the rest to the trash-can. I became a little demoralized, as my hope again had not come to fruition once again.

Thirty-two years old and still a complete loser, I was furious with life, but yet again, I wasn't going to give up.

Shortly after this, I was randomly offered a position as a negotiator in a real estate business from a friend who was the newly promoted manager. I had never previously believed that I was good enough to get a job position like that. A few years earlier, I wanted to apply for a negotiator position in a real estate office when painting inside. Still, I thought I would be wasting my time as to why they would employ a loser like me.

So after the formal interview for the job, I was still hesitant to take the job due to my self-belief issues. Still, with some persuasion, I decided to give it a go. I had a family to feed, and the lure of a company car meant that I no longer needed to worry about push starting my car every day, which I had been doing for months.

I've had some rough cars in my time; one car rolled down a slope while I was putting fuel into the tank. Fortunately, I just managed to stop it before it went into a busy road. It was quite the stretch but not as long as the stretch I would have received had I of killed someone. On another occasion, I had come out of my home one afternoon to find my car 200 yards down the street cuddled up to someone else's car. Now there is nothing wrong with a bit of car-love, but my car was way too enthusiastic. The wheel was hanging off, and there was damage to the other vehicle, which unfortunately happened to be owned by a grumpy neighbor. I had to knock his door and tell him which was a painful moment. If only I had been insured it would have been so much easier.

I really could write a book just on car incidents that I have had. Anyway, I was excited to get a new car, wear a suit to work, and feel respectable. I was on the up.

After three months of working six days a week from 8.30 am to 8 pm and giving absolutely everything, I had a few offers but not sold one single property. I was in despair, as selling property is not difficult. You have people looking and you have people selling, so you just treat it like a game of snap. You show everyone every property until you get a match, but even that seemed to elude me, and so again, I wondered that I should quit and go back to painting, where I would earn money, rather than relying on a commission that I was not making. Then what seemed like almost overnight, something changed, a deal that I had been working on came in, and then another, it rained property sales. Those moments were joyous. For the first time in my miserable life, I had achieved some success. I even won the monthly sales award as the South East of England's best negotiator and from one of the company's smallest offices. Prior to that I had never won a single thing throughout my life, not even so much as a raffle ticket. I also received a small bonus and a promotion to the position of a senior negotiator. For the very first time in my life, I felt as if I was someone. I went from looser to legend.

Just eighteen months later, I quit the real estate agency and opened my own with a colleague, borrowing 5K from a loan shark. Borrowing from a loan shark wasn't the smartest of moves, but it was the only option at the time. As long as we had the monthly money to pay back, I would be OK, right?

It was upsetting having to return my company car and return back to a cheap old car, but at the same time, I was excited to be starting my own real estate company. After just a few weeks of owning this car, I again needed to push start the car every time I wanted to use it. I would look for hills to park everywhere I went. And it smoked like a burning oil drum. I used to have to wash the back of it, so I didn't get my suit dirty.

The business was a struggle as the competition was fierce, with my competitors throwing eye-watering amounts of money into their marketing. We could not compete. The partnership with my colleague split after a short period, and it was agreed that I would keep the business and the debts. One morning I received a letter from the bank to say that the cheque I had written to cover the rent and the admin secretary's wages had bounced. Not knowing what to do and hugely concerned, I pondered that I might be out of business. I had no idea what to do. Later that evening, I visited a family member at her apartment for a cuppa and a chat. As I walked into the building's foyer and feeling dejected, I noticed a sign on a front door of a ground floor apartment that read, Jesus, will save you. Not being religious, I laughed under my breath, muttering – "that would be good, yeah cool, if you could do that for me please, oh and throw in a new car as well please," as I proceeded up the stairs. I explained what had happened. Marie told me that she had received a loan payment for some new windows a few months away from being installed and offered to loan me the money if I could pay her back within 6 weeks. After deliberating for less than a nanosecond, I accepted. I was shocked, relieved, and so happy that I did a little dance around the kitchen. Ivan Rose had another shot and was be able to pay the rent and wages. However, I was still faced with not being able to compete with nine competitors and knew that this would be an on going issue.

At the time, my admin secretary told me that she had previously completed a course on rental management and that she still had the work manuals at home. I immediately asked to borrow them from her. I took some time reading and studying them and decided my best move was to quit the sale and concentrate on rentals. It was a risky decision because all the other rental companies were in the city center. No one had opened a rental business in the suburbs of the city before. But I had nothing to lose, and so I went for it. It turned out to be the best move I could have made. All of a sudden, competitors became my allies, using me as leverage to sell rental properties to investors. They would send their customers to me for rental values and investment reassurance. Business went from strength to strength.

Although fraught with confrontation and challenges, I had created a very profitable business, opening my second branch a couple of years later. Over twelve years, I became more and more successful. I acquired all the material possessions that I had ever dreamed of; a beautiful gated home, an Aston Martin car, and even a boat.

Always wanting to make others happy, I would take friends and families on holidays and trips.

In January 2010, I took a vacation to Florida with my Mother and Aunt, where I unexpectedly found myself a girlfriend. I started traveling back and forth to spend time with her as she had a young child and a complicated situation with her ex-husband. Initially, things were great, but there was massive drama between her and her ex-husband; it was out and out war and one giant control and custody battle. After a while, her anger shifted on to me. I tried all I could do to help. I pleaded with her to cut down her alcohol consumption but doing this made things worse. I found myself the enemy, and before I knew it, I had become the victim of alcohol-fuelled domestic abuse. Running homes in both the UK and in the US, contributing towards her legal costs and other financial commitments I had undertaken, caused my finances to take a dive. Over time, my overhead became higher than my income, and money had gotten tight. When the money ran out, the love went with it, and I was stuck on a roller coaster of chaos, drama, and confrontation. On several occasions, I had been thrown out or walked out in the middle of the night. I had nowhere to go, which was not a good situation, especially in another country.

A friend of mine, understanding of my situation, kindly loaned me a car that he wasn't using. Knowing how unpredictable she was, I hid a blanket and pillow in the trunk, as I knew that I would more than likely end up needing it, which of course I did. A few weeks later, the license plates had expired. The required document for renewal was given to me when I was first loaned the car but mysteriously went missing from where I had left them. I searched everywhere and suspected foul play, but not finding them meant that I couldn't legally drive the car, so I had to leave the car on the driveway.

A few days later, I had returned to the UK when another drama unfolded in an episode of drunken outrage. She had called my friend demanding he moved his car from the driveway and was very rude to him and his wife. After hanging up the phone, she proceeded to call a tow company and had his vehicle towed off and scrapped. To make things worse, she took a picture of the car when on the tow truck's back and sent it to us both. A few months later, I returned to the US, and while I was changing flights was told that a friend of hers whom I had never met would be meeting me at the airport to bring me home. I figured that she wanted to have a drink and, therefore, could not drive.

When I arrived home, she was drunk and half asleep in the chair. I hadn't seen her for months and, of course, was extremely disappointed. Within the hour, another night of full-on drama erupted, and I endured hours of verbal abuse. The next morning, when she took her daughter to school, I packed my belongings as fast as possible and walked out. I did not know where to go or what to do, so I headed to the local coffee shop to get free Wi-Fi, as my cell phone would only work when in the UK. I was in a bit of a state, having had hardly any sleep and feeling pretty down. I was also in tremendous pain with my knee, which required surgery, and I should have had done several years earlier. So with great difficultly, I limped for three miles dragging my suitcase, acquiring four huge blisters on each foot. I couldn't believe it, fifty years old, homeless in America, with just 10 bucks to my name. It was hard to comprehend.

During my five years back and forth to the US, I had somehow managed to switch my financial status from a worth above $1.5m to finding myself $200,000 in debt. I lost my business and virtually all of my material possessions, which I had slowly sold off to keep the lifestyle going. I came home, totally embarrassed, with my pride and confidence in tatters.

Before leaving the US, my good friend, who had helped me out many times, introduced me to a chap called Tom. After learning of my situation, the latter offered me a position working in his import business in the UK. And No, it wasn't importing drugs; it was and still is a proper, reputable, and very successful company.

Upon my return and to start work, I relocated 250 miles from my hometown, moving into a dingy shared house. Within ten days of starting work, I became sick and ended up having emergency surgery for appendicitis. Tom and I got on very well from day one, and we developed a great friendship. His wisdom and guidance shaped my future. For that, I am forever grateful for as I am also to my close friends Dave and Rachel, for their help and support during those difficult times I experienced in the US.

Although grateful for the employment, I was not enjoying the job. The office atmosphere was uncomfortable and frosty. I dreaded going to work. Still licking my wounds from the past few years and having some internal struggles, I decided to seek a hypnotherapist.

In searching for a therapist, I unexpectedly stumbled across a hypnotherapy diploma course that was due to commence the following month. Up until that point, I thought a dip -loma was an Italian sex act. I had always been interested in hypnotherapy. The thought of actually learning about this subject excited me; I knew that it was the right thing to do. So without hesitation and as eager as a dog on heat, I applied, took the interview, passed the test, and enrolled on the course, loving every minute of the learning. My journey of change had commenced.

A year later, after completing the hypnotherapy course, I quit my job and had my long-awaited knee surgery. Like a deranged greyhound with his tail on fire, I was out of there.

Back in my home town of Southampton, I suffered another personal setback. Again finding myself broken-hearted after a long-distance relationship did not work out. It hit me pretty bad. I had no income, substantial debt, without a job, no car, and recovering from knee surgery, accessorized with a full leg brace, which I wore for eight weeks. Things were not going well, and I was down. I had got to the point that I didn't care whether I lived or died. Frankly, I thought life was absolute garbage. I was living alone in a timber-converted shed without windows, heating, or even a bed. No matter how hard I tried, I couldn't turn the tide. I have to say that hiding from debt collectors when you don't have any windows does make things a little easier. Still, I was at my wits' end and then kicked in the nomads yet again when some thieving piece of crap stole my bicycle from right under my nose. I would joke; listen, I didn't get to where I am today by being smart -OK. Unable to find direction and to calm my anxiety, I began meditating like a Buddhist monk on temazepam, sometimes for up to 4 hours a day, searching and questioning. I didn't realize it at the time, but I was entering into a period of unintentional self –isolation.

During a meditation one morning, I recalled a vision that I had some years earlier. It was a vision that started with seeing a small shadow in the corner of the baseboard. As I looked harder, I noticed that I could see the outline of the back of a person. As I looked hard again, it started growing bigger and bigger, and then it turned around. I could see a roman gladiator, holding a shield and wielding a sword in full costume. The more I focused, the clearer the face became, and to my astonishment, I saw that it was my face. A thought came loud and clear into my mind; You can achieve and manifest anything you desire if you want it enough. After the meditation, the message lingered in my thoughts, and I pondered on it for the rest of the day. I meditated again on this thought later that evening and concluded that the changes I truly needed would need enormous. It would need to encompass many aspects of my life Emotionally, Spiritually, Mentally, Physically, and Financially.

Emotionally- because I had was easily hurt and knew that I needed to be more emotionally stable.

Spiritually, because I figured out that connecting with our higher self is the gateway to manifestation, faith, and guidance. The better the connection, the better the result.

Mentally- because I wanted clarity of thought and direction, to feel self-assured and positive, be free thinking, and in control of my life.

Physically- because I want to be in good health, enjoy physical pleasures, and to feel good about myself.

Financially- because I have learned that being in good financial shape determines our life quality. I wanted financial freedom to live my best experience on my terms and the ability to help others.

I have always believed that we must give to receive. As a child, I used to ask for success in return for helping others; I was trying to make a deal with God. Remembering this, I decided to list what I wanted and created a vision board. Starting with a large piece of paper, I drew pictures of what I wanted to achieve with a coded message in writing alongside so that only I would know what it meant. I framed it and hung it on the wall, where it still is today. Then I created an affirmation; - I am in alignment with the laws of the universe. The laws of the universe are in alignment with me, which I continue to repeat every day. Before I knew it, things started to change, and I was somehow being guided. I had several months earlier started a business selling wholesale plantation shutters, but my direction just stopped. It felt like I jumped off a train and onto another passing by without any knowledge of the direction I would be going in. I suddenly felt compelled to study. I don't even like studying, but at that moment, I decided to ditch the shutter business and pursue my passion for helping others. It was no longer about just trying to make a buck; it was now much bigger than that.

I had always felt my life purpose was to help others, and I did become a Samaritan's counselor when I was in my twenties. I did this for about a year but quit when I noticed that my problems were worse than most callers. It dawned on me that I was on the wrong end of the phone.

After refreshing my hypnotherapy knowledge, I progressed on some different practices. I studied hypno-analysis, cognitive behavioral therapy (CBT), Child psychology, Havening, Neuro-linguistic programming (NLP), Eye movement desensitization, and reprocessing (EMDR). And anything I could find regarding mental health. I became obsessed, spending ten months alone in my converted shed, barely venturing outside, other than a grocery store trip. In between study, I would meditate. In the evenings, I would write comedy, poetry, short stories, or daydream rather than watching TV.

During this time, I developed a strong sense of belief that amazing things were going to happen. I had lost a lot of the fear I was holding and felt ready to take on the world. I was prepared to share my knowledge, experiences, learnings, and intuition to inspire and teach others. I knew that anyone who could learn could also create a dramatic and positive change with help.

Things started to change fast, and I soon noticed that my manifestation drawings had begun to materialize. Through a chance encounter, I was offered work in practice as a hypnotherapist, which I duly accepted. I had no practical experience, but whenever I was presented with an issue or wasn't sure what to do, the solution just came to me. I was able to read into people's feelings and needs with surety and confidence. I started to achieve incredible results in improving their mental health using my unique style, which I tailored for each client. The practice gave me a never-ending supply and mixture of clients from factory workers to high-ranking military or police personal. The compliments, gifts, cards, referrals, and reviews showed me that I had something unique going on. The biggest surprise of all was my ability to get great results with children. I mean, I have always liked them and raised two wonderful sons of my own, but I never envisaged working with them. The practice noticed this quickly and was so impressed that they would send all child clients to me. I was surprised by the results.

Curing phobias, anxiety, and fear-based issues developing their confidence, and most importantly, getting them to go to school, which is a big problem for many children suffering from anxiety or behavioral disorder. In most instances, I would work with the parents to teach them to behave in specific ways. I have often wondered if the difficulty I faced as a child allowed me to relate to how these children were thinking and feeling. - Anyway, whatever the reason - it works, and I am grateful.

Top tip; The best time to help a child suffering from anxiety-related disorders is before puberty. A child receiving help at this age will avoid many struggles, both as a teenager and an adult.

All children of this age would hugely benefit from having a therapy session to clear stored emotions regardless of their upbringing. We all have them from our childhood experiences, whether it is inside or outside the home. No one escapes traumatic experiences. A clearance therapy sets them up as adults bringing them a well-balanced and calm mindset.

In this chapter, I have shared a few of the many challenges that I have endured. And so now, I would like to encourage you to take a moment to consider how you feel after reading this?

Did it motivate or inspire you? What emotions, if any, resonate with you?

Overall did it make you feel Negative or Positive? How does it relate to your challenges and experiences?

When I reflect on my past, I see; Humor in memory, Learning in mistakes, Strength in weakness, Determination in failure, and Motivation in adversity. I certainly feel no sadness; I recognize that this is the life chosen to gain my life experience and give me the spiritual growth I need.

I noticed a definite theme that has been with me for all of my life. And that is, if you knock me down, I'm coming back stronger because giving up never has and will never be an option for me. I will achieve my goals and desires, or I will die trying. Emotional and physical hardship has enabled me to find my life purpose. It has helped me understand and to help others in a way I could never have done. All of my previous experiences have led me to where I am today.

Through adversity and against the odds, I have turned my life around and found a great life purpose. I have found an abundance of love, many friendships, a career that I'm passionate about, and personal fulfillment. I laugh daily, and my creativity flows for the most part on demand. That doesn't mean that I do not have difficulties, challenges, or things go wrong because this is a part of everyone's life. It means; I manage my feelings, believe I can overcome any obstacle, and work to manifest my desires and dreams to come true. Most importantly, to the best of my ability, I control my life and live my life on my terms.

You, too, can overcome any situation and achieve the things you desire. If I can do it, so can you. Whatever has gone before you, or whatever you have lost, no one can take away what you have between your ears. You have memories, learnings, and experiences, which are exclusively yours forever, to use anywhere, anytime, for a better life experience.

Chapter 3

Matters of the Mind

Overthinking or worrying is a bill you do not need to pay

Several years ago, I used to see this chap literately every time I went to the gym. His name was Pat, and I wondered if he worked in security as he swaggered around like he owned the place. Pat resembled a Staffordshire bull terrier in build but with smaller ears. He had a massive muscular body with a neck like an oak tree and was littered with tattoos. His shaved head and stubble face reminded me of a pineapple. On a few occasions, I tried to acknowledge him with a half-smile and a head nod. Each time he ignored me, which made me feel uncomfortable.

One evening I decided to go into the sauna, and there he was again, sat alone. As I entered, he gave me what I perceived as a bit of a snarl, and I could tell instantly that he wasn't a man who used botox. I shuffled past, feeling a little intimidated, and sat down opposite him where and minded my own business. The silence felt awkward, and so it was either offer him a treat and tell him "who's a good boy" or say something intellectual. Instead, I said something utterly ridiculous. I said, "It's hot in here, isn't it"? He smirked at my silly comment, and it worked out to be an excellent icebreaker, or should I say heat breaker. Anyway, we started chatting, and I found him very amiable.

After speaking a while, I found out that he and his wife Kay had recently lost their 21-year-old son a few months earlier. And so I learned that my perception of him not liking me was completely wrong, and in my head. I was jumping to conclusions based on his appearance. I felt terrible for his loss and helped him with some subtle talk therapy and on the spot counseling.

A while later, I bumped into him in the gym; he was chasing the ball, which had rolled away. He seemed more upbeat. My ears pricked up when he told me that he was a security dog trainer and that the name of his business was; Pineapple Kaynine.

We were both on our way to a yoga class, and so we went walkies together; it was a sweet moment, mostly when we did the downward dog pose in unison. It was nice to see that he was beginning to heal, and we became good friends.

A man's best friend is often a dog.

Fortunately, I have since learned to stay open-minded until evidence, truth, or fact is established. The bottom line is that judging anyone or anything by appearance or opinion alone is always a mistake and often leads us into a false belief. When we over-analyze, over-worry, or over-think, we will develop fantasized fear. Our imaginations run wild when we visualize the worst scenarios or outcomes, believing they will happen. Whenever we engage in this, we are merely guessing or predicting an outcome, which is almost always wrong. When we think or predict, we not only waste our time but cause unnecessary anxiety and stress. And all because of an entirely futile thought that has no facts or evidence. To act upon something that isn't true will affect your life's direction, and others too—ensuring that there is sufficient proof is essential before we act. If we have no evidence, then we should dismiss it and either let it go or search for more, but never should we judge based on opinion or gut feeling.

It is absolutely astonishing that millions of people worldwide are making life-changing decisions based on a hunch, a guess, or a prediction. Because of that, it will be mostly wrong. When observing successful businesses, the military, law, education, health care, and the government do not use emotion when making decisions. Instead, they rely on facts and evidence.

Nothing ever happens the same twice because no two situations are precisely the same. When something negative has occurred with symmetry to the previous occurrence, it is easy to believe it will happen again. Actually, it is less likely to happen again. Our minds are programmed to protect us and always search for ways to avoid a repeat of a bad experience. Let's say you fell over and hurt yourself or lost something; your mind questions and searches for why it happened. The next time you are in that place or situation again, you will naturally be more cautious, having learned your lesson from the previous experience.

If we know that something negative will happen, you will either not do it or change something about it to limit the damage.

When we remember the past times, our memories will have become deleted and distorted. We only remember aspects of a memory. Ask yourself what you were wearing or had for dinner three weeks ago last Tuesday? Unless a significant event occurred, you would struggle to remember. That's just one memory in one day and not even that long ago. Perhaps you have looked at a photo of yourself smiling and looking happy. Still, when you stopped to think about it, you remembered that you were not happy at that moment.

When something has happened, it can never un-happen. There is nothing you can do to change past events, but you can change the way you view them. Our memories are affected by the way we think in the now. If we remember events negatively, it will cause us to react negatively to new similar situations.

We all have many core beliefs from the learnings and the experiences we have had in childhood. These beliefs impact our behavior as adults. The problem is that many of these beliefs we have learned are false. For instance; If a dog bit you as a child, you may believe that all dogs will bite you, which of course, is not true as you will have encountered many dogs that have not bitten you. And there are many examples of this type of false core belief learning. Our belief system is totally dependant on those that guide us, and the situations we experience.

Our belief systems are also influenced not only by our peers and experiences but from many aspects of society. Advertisers and the media have been manipulating our belief systems for the whole of our lives. We can also become terribly influenced by old wives' tales, such as; you can wash your hands, but you can't wash your mind. These types of sayings often promote fear. Some are for safety purposes, and others are superstition. Whatever you have been told in the past does not mean that it is accurate, so you should not automatically believe. We can all experience what is known as "Illusory correlation." Our brain plays tricks on us leading us to believe something to be true that is not true.

For instance, a gambler remembers the wins and not the losses. Regardless of how much has been lost, the gambler believes that he will likely win the next bet. A person who has a bad experience in a restaurant claims the restaurant to be substandard, even though he has happily eaten there many times before. Another person may have had an unpleasant experience with someone on holiday and came home complaining about how awful the people of that country were. This type of biased thinking is a contributing factor to racism and European football hooliganism.

We all analyze and worry about certain things; it's natural. Too much-worrying empties today of its strength, but a little worry is both healthy and necessary for us. Without it, we would otherwise lack urgency or action, which could compromise our safety and wellbeing. There is, of course, a big difference between a healthy worry and overly worrying.

Top tip; Examine your beliefs using evidence, facts, and truth only, instead of feelings, opinions, and ideas. Remember, every situation is different. Even if it has similarities to a previous, it is still likely to have a different outcome.

If you are unsure about a situation's truth or the feeling you have, create yourself an imaginary jury to evaluate by presenting evidence from both sides. (For and Against) This way, you can determine if there is overwhelming proof or not.

When things have not worked out for you, analyze what part you played in it. When you know the role you played in the outcome, you will have learned something about yourself. And you will be better able to accept the situation and manage similar situations better in the future.

Acceptance

Often things happen that we have no control over, but we can control how we react. Acceptance is vital for moving on. The longer it takes to accept what has happened, the more stuck you will become. No matter what has happened, when something negative occurs, you must immediately acknowledge the situation for what it is, regardless of how disappointing or upsetting you find it. Until you do this, you will be unable to focus on a solution or achieve a resolution. Many become paralyzed in disbelief or blame, which serves no definite purpose other than to deepen the anguish and stall the recovery process. As soon as we accept a situation, we can focus on what we can do to fix it. There may be no solution in some circumstances, but you will move forward as long as you find acceptance. When we are powerless to an outcome or situation, we must recognize it. If we do not let go of a problem that we cannot win, it will likely worsen. Recognizing when you can't fight the force and accepting and letting go as soon as possible is always best. Instead, make the best of the situation by focusing on damage limitation rather than self-destruction. You can tell yourself - perhaps it just wasn't meant to be.

Taking things personally

When we take negative comments personally, it affects us emotionally. If someone is continuously critiquing you without justification, it cannot be because of you; it will be because you are in the wrong place at the wrong time. That person is venting his or her frustration towards you. Those who frequently put others down are likely insecure and have low self-esteem, causing that person frustration, anger, or jealousy.

If someone rejects you for what seems like no reason, it means something is going within that other person you are not aware of, and again it is not about you. Our thoughts, behavior, and words come from our own beliefs. Those accusing others of being dishonest or deceitful without evidence are doing so because that is how their minds work. Those that think deceptively or dishonestly are.

Top tip; If you are a victim of someone who is always putting you down, then do your best to stay away from them. Still, if that is not possible, maintaining minimum contact is your best option. Suppose you could challenge the person who is being critical by asking them to explain precisely what was meant by their comments so that you could consider the evidence. Understanding what was exactly meant by the words used will help you determine if it's true. If it is not, you dismiss it. If it is, you take it as constructive criticism, affording you the opportunity for self-improvement. So, there is never a need to worry about critical comments.

Expectation

Whenever we place too much expectation on others or ourselves, we are very likely to experience a ton of disappointment. Suppose we expect too much from ourselves and continuously feel like nothing we do is good enough even though we are trying our best. In that case, we are likely perfectionists. Perfectionists think that nothing they do is ever good enough. Know that perfectionism is an unrealistic expectation and that having too high expectations will always let you down.

Even the most skilled people commonly make errors; they are called mistakes, and we all make them; it's how we learn and improve that's important. Achieving the best result comes from practice, learning, and effort, not from an unrealistic expectation to be brilliant at everything. You may be abundant with natural talent, but you still need to practice an awful lot to be very good at something. Practicing is everything; the more you practice, the better you get. Reducing expectations in your self and others allows you to feel more satisfied. This doesn't mean that it's ok to do a substandard job or that you don't want the best outcome, but we have to have a realistic expectation. Each and everyone on the planet can only do their best, and so if you are a perfectionist, you must first recognize that you are and know that your best is always good enough. How can your best not be good enough if it is the best you can do? You can always strive to do better the next time.

The Present Moment

Jackie and Dan had been married for 9 years and shared a daughter called Mary. Dan was easy-going and tolerant of Jackie, who was dominant and regimented. Shortly after they had got together, Dan decided to pour a bath for them to share, lighting candles to make the occasion as romantic as possible. After about 10 minutes, Jackie jumped out, telling Dan that she would go put a towel in the drier. He thought this to be a very thoughtful gesture until he realized that she had only put one towel in the drier, and it was for her. Stating, "I'm not your slave."

She would compare everything to past events and always reminded Dan of his past failings too. She would openly compare him to previous partners, of which he could never measure up to. It wasn't unusual for her to belittle him in front of others and had thrown him out on several occasions.

Dan was just 5 feet tall, and Jackie regularly joked that she had bought him a child booster seat for Christmas so that he could see over the steering wheel in their motor home. Eventually, enough was enough, and so one weekend after being thrown out yet again, he decided not to return.

Jackie had been living on her own for a few months and missed Dan. Each time he came to pick up Mary, she would remind him of the fantastic relationship he had thrown away, trying to lure him back in. Feeling lonely and dwelling on past times, Jackie started to trawl through social media, looking to reconnect with old friends, even setting up a group with those she knew from school. She had arranged to reunite with some old friends at a local bar on the following Thursday.

Arriving early, she bought herself a drink and waited patiently. After 30 minutes or so, Valarie showed. She was expecting four of her school friends, but no one else showed.

Jackie and Valerie spent the evening chatting about the old days, the friends that didn't show, and their life stories to date. Valerie had a bit of a coughing fit after a drink going down the wrong way, and her false teeth accidentally flew out of her mouth and onto the bar. Embarrassed, she profoundly apologized, explaining, "These teeth are a bit loose, I borrowed them from my Mother, but at least I didn't lose them this time.

"You borrowed your Mothers false teeth?" Jackie reaffirmed in shock.

"Yes, and if I lose them, I am really in deep trouble as these are new and not cheap, by the way; I lost her other set last week. So I met this guy and ended up staying in his motor home. I had a few drinks, and in the morning I couldn't find them. I was running late as I had to take my youngest to school, but when I returned to the layby where we stayed a few hours later, he was gone, and I never saw him nor my Mother's teeth again.

My Mother and I had a challenging conversation when I got home as neither of us had any teeth, and she was furious; it was like a lisp fest. Well, because of that, she didn't want to loan them to me tonight. This is why I was a little late; I had to wait for Mom to have her supper first. She made me promise to keep them in my mouth this time because she said that she could not bear to live on soup again for a week. Anyway, the good news is that I will be getting my new teeth in a few days; I'm having my implants fitted. Jackie complained that her teeth were also in need of a lot of work, but she couldn't afford it due to her husband leaving. During the conversation, Jackie was surprised to discover that Valeria happened to be good friends with her neighbor and new friend, Gloria.

The next morning, Gloria coyly asked Jackie how the reunion went. Jackie explained, "Only Valeria showed and how different she was to how I remembered her. She looked well, though, apart from her teeth, and she knows you, Gloria? What a coincidence."

"Yes, I used to work with her. In fact, we are meeting up tomorrow for a coffee."

A week previous, Jackie was chatting to Gloria when her brother Rob showed up. Jackie instantly liked him and later told Gloria how he reminded her of an ex-lover that she wished she married. Gloria explained that Rob had been single for over two years and that she would pass her comments on to him.

Gloria spoke with Rob the following day and told him that Jackie was interested in him.

Rob decided to make a surprise visit to his sister's hoping to see Jackie. Still, it just so happened to be the evening Jackie had gone to meet Valarie. A little disappointed, Rob left Gloria's early and went home. Jackie was disappointed too and asked Gloria to arrange for Rob to visit again soon.

Gloria and Valerie met at the coffee shop opposite the dentist, where Valerie had just had her new teeth fitted. While Gloria and Valerie were chatting, Rob walked in for a coffee. Gloria exclaimed, "that's my brother," and called him over; Valarie's exclaimed, "that's my dentist," Yes, call him over, please.

Upon leaving, Valerie and Rob exchanged contact details, which led to a met up that weekend.

The following week Mary had come home from visiting her Dad with a set of false teeth in her hand, which she found rather amusing. Asking where they had come from, Mary said that she had seen them in her Dad's motor home. Jackie realized that Valerie must have been with Dan the night she lost her teeth. Angry, she stomped to Gloria's house and explained what had happened. Gloria reminded Jackie that she and Dan were separated. She also told her that Valerie and Rob had met at the coffee shop and were now dating. Then she inadvertently mentioned that Rob was a dentist. Jackie's jaw hit the floor, things going from bad to worse was Devasted to learn this, so she called Valerie and asked her to come over.

When she arrived, Jackie confronted her, showing her the teeth, asking if they belonged to her Mother. Valerie was a little taken back and, after a quick examination, confirmed that they did belong to her Mother, asking how Jackie acquired them. She told her, "they were found in my husband's motor home."

"Oh dear, I had no idea that he was your husband; he said he had been single for over a month, and actually, you told me that you were single?"

Gloria stepped in to calm things down, confirming that to be true.

Jackie then offered Valerie her teeth back, saying, "Here you are, take these teeth back to your Mother.

Valerie replied, "Mother has new and better ones now, so you can throw them in the trash. They are in the past now.

Upset, Jackie went into the kitchen, and Valeria and Gloria left.

Once Valerie had gone home, Gloria went to check in on Jackie. She sat Jackie down and held her hand. "Can I be honest with you, Jackie? I am really sorry everything has gone like this, but Dan is your ex. You lost him because you valued your previous partners more than him. You missed out on meeting Rob because you were hell-bent on creating a reunion to meet people you haven't seen in over 20 years. I helped you by arranging for Valerie to go to the reunion as she told me that she didn't think the others were going to show. They have moved on and are getting on with their lives. They like us are different people now. I've noticed that since we have met, you are constantly living in the past; I have tried to help you as much as I can. When you spend your life in the past, you miss out on the now. And the now is critical for setting up your future. You need to let go and move on; otherwise, you will never find that happiness you are searching for."

Our happiness does not come by dwelling on the past; it comes from the now. Our only actual reality is now, as the future hasn't happened, and the past has gone. We can never feel truly content if we are always somewhere else in our minds. It can be enjoyable to look back into our past, but I believe we should only do this if they are positive memories. Unless it's for a specific purpose or learning, there should never be a reason to ponder on negative experiences from the past. All it will do will make you miserable unless, of course, you want to feel sad. So unless that is the case, leave the past in the past.

Remember, things continuously evolve and change. So when we make plans for the future, we should not look too far ahead because anything can happen. Things always work out differently from how we expect. Making loose plans for our long-term future and firm plans for our immediate future is excellent as we all need to have things to look forward to and work towards. The most crucial time is now because what we do today affects tomorrow. Notice how children naturally live in the present moment. This is the key to their level of happiness and acceptance, which is why they recover from situations so quickly, moving to the next position as if the previous didn't happen. As we grow up, we tend to lose this ability, which makes our lives more complicated. It is all about the here and now.

Life will give you whatever experience is most helpful for the evolution of your consciousness. How do you know this is the experience you need? Because this is the experience you are having at the moment." ***Eckhart Tolle***

Practice; This to help you tune in to the present moment

1. Spend two minutes gazing at an object or a candle flame. Keep your eyes and mind focused on the item or flame, and study the detail.

2. Then, take a moment to tune into your heartbeat. With your eyes closed, listen, and feel your heart beating in your chest for about a minute.

3. Spend five minutes examining things either outdoors in nature or objects and items around your home or office. Attentively examine everything in great detail, noticing things that you would usually not see, using your senses of sight, touch, and smell. Be close so you can look closely at the textures, formations, patterns, colors, and workings.

Phobia and Avoidance

A phobia is an overwhelming fear of a place, situation, object, or living creature. Millions of people worldwide suffer from a phobia, and many have more than one. Phobias are fixable, and yet a high percentage of sufferers do not get help. An overwhelming experience can cause us to develop an irrational fear, which causes us to believe that the worst outcome will occur. All phobias are anxiety-related and often developed in childhood. Sometimes we might not remember the event itself. However, it would have been a standout experience at the time. Phobia symptoms are feelings of extreme fear and often accompanied by panic attacks, dizziness, or breathing difficulties.

When the phobia becomes a panic attack, many people believe that they will faint, have a heart attack, or endure some other terrifying outcome, even death. Although extremely unpleasant, a panic attack is only a fear-based thought, and no harm is likely to happen. When we become terrified and overly concerned about an outcome, we can start to shallow breath, which causes tightening of the chest and then dizziness due to hyperventilating. The best thing to do is keep your airways open and regulate your breathing to control the panic attack.

If you have a phobia, then you have an anxiety disorder. That anxiety disorder can very often have other anxiety outlets. You will know this by observing your behavior. For instance, if you have been cured of a phobia and develop another or have more than one phobia. Maybe you drink too much, smoke, bite, or pick your nails. If you have a phobia and overthink or analyze too much, become frustrated quickly, or suffer low moods. In this case, the phobia you are experiencing is just a part of overall anxiety. With phobia comes avoidance. When you use avoidance, you strengthen the fear's power, making you more likely to avoid more situations. Avoiding situations will make you feel worse, mostly when avoiding things that need to be done. This will further lower your self-esteem and confidence. By avoiding situations, you are potentially creating a much bigger problem that may end up out of your control, which will make matters even worse. If you are not working towards improvement - you will be going backward because anxiety doesn't stay still; it manifests. There is, of course, positive types of avoidance. Still, the difference is that positive avoidance is not based on an irrational fear but caution, common sense, and self-preservation.

Practice; When trying to do something challenging that you have previously avoided, it is better to break down the steps into achievable targets - even if they are small. Taking dolly steps and moving towards your goal will boost you with a feel-good factor and means that you are progressing. (Try the two-minute rule) Don't be frightened to ask for help because it's always beneficial to have support. Know that those who offer you help or assistance feel rewarded in your acceptance; they want to help you; otherwise, they wouldn't have offered, and it doesn't matter why someone wants to help you.

To calculate how severe your phobia is, you should create a SUD score (subjective unit of distress score). A SUD score should be between one and ten. One being the lowest, and ten the highest. Phobia is an irrational fear that has a connection to a healthy fear. For instance, heights can be dangerous, as can a spider bite. So it makes perfect sense to have a healthy fear toward something that can harm you, but with phobias, we have developed an over-inflated fear. A typical SUD score for those who do not have any phobia should be around 2-3 or less, and so the higher your SUD score is, the stronger the phobia.

If you have a phobia with a SUD score of over three, please listen to **Hypnosis audio download 004 Phobia cure** *to get this issue resolved.*

Decision-making

When making big decisions and by that, I mean decisions with life-changing implications such as breaking up with a partner or changing your job. Think through carefully, where you are going? What exactly are you doing, and why are you doing it? What are the implications of your actions? And is the timing, right? We can easily make decisions when fed up or upset only to feel very different when we have calmed down. Realizing that we have made a colossal mistake can be very regrettable. The majority of us tend to make too many decisions based on emotion, especially with generic advice such as; go with your gut feeling. There is some truth in this, but a gut feeling alone can often be wrong and requires additional evidence-based information. We all make the wrong decision sometimes. When this happens, we may feel remorseful. Still, we should never regret a conclusion as we made the best decision we could, given the circumstances and choices we had at that time. We are unable to turn back the clock.

When taking advice from those that we know, bear in mind that those giving advice see it from their perspective and not yours. Suppose several people are saying the same thing. In that case, it might be a warning to pay more attention to the situation, so way up the facts so you can make an informed decision. When asking for third party advice, be sure to ask a person with substantial knowledge or expertise in that subject or have evidence to support what they have said. You shouldn't ask for financial advice from someone with a gambling addiction.

Suppose you struggle to make small decisions that will not or are unlikely to affect tomorrow, next week, next month, or next year. It means that you have too much self-doubt going on and are likely to be overthinking it or being overly concerned about getting the answer wrong. Being in two minds causes even more self-doubt. It is always better to be decisive rather than hesitating for too long. If it turns out to be inaccurate, you can change your mind later. If that's not possible, you will have learned something for the next time you are in that situation, which will be more decisive.

I have listed some things to consider and help you make better choices. Gut feeling, desire, financial implications, practicality, legality, physical risk, availability, logistics, risk, reward, best and worst outcome, short and long-term implications, health, family, and friends.

Practice; Try this visualization technic for making a decision.

Take a moment and imagine a long piece of wood over an abyss of water. Metaphorically attach your choices to each end, and visualize the plank sinking into the sea. You can only save one side, and this will be your answer. You can do this with several sides if you choose, but you can only save one. Or imagine that it was a best friend or close family member of yours asking, What would you advise them to do? If you still can't decide, then perhaps no decision is the right decision. If you are still unable to determine your decision, you can use meditation or seek professional advice.

Procrastination is a particular issue for those who are insecure. If we are in a procrastination state, then we are stagnant, but others will perceive us as weak, lazy, and going nowhere in life. Successful people do not procrastinate for long. They are proactive, reactive, and decisive. People like this are more successful but are much more appealing to others. They recognize the importance of time and carry out swift action when necessary, knowing that they can review their decisions whenever they feel appropriate. Doing this allows them to move onto the next decision, rather than becoming stuck on one particular matter. Good decision-makers know that they can always revisit a decision when or if other facts come to light.

Top tip; If we do not feel like doing a task that needs to be done, apply the two-minute rule. List the jobs that need to be done daily and spend two minutes minimum on each. Following this two-minute rule will promote feelings of satisfaction and help de-clutter your mind, which allows you to progress toward your goals. Doing something for just two minutes can inspire you to carry on for longer, and if you do, then the rewards for you will likely be even higher.

Anxiety

Anxiety is environmental, genetic, and learned behavior. If you suffer from an anxiety-related disorder, the likelihood is that at least one of your parents has also experienced an anxiety disorder. Conquering fear is about building rapport within. We can develop confidence and self-esteem by clearing the past, developing internal-love, and improving our cognitive thinking. When we do this, we learn self-trust and self-assurance, and we eliminate self-doubt. In your mind, unless you motorize your thoughts, there are no consequences to your thinking, and as far as I'm aware, there are no laws that govern our review, so think freely without guilt. Be free to fantasize, dream, and explore your mind.

Because every emotion has a motion, if you are experiencing anxiety, you will have physical symptoms. Perhaps you bite or pick your nails, jiggle your legs, have sleep issues, grind your teeth in your sleep, or become angry or frustrated quickly. Emotions also motorize our behaviors, actions, and habits, so it is so vital that we learn to manage our emotions well. When we have experienced something profoundly upsetting or traumatic, our subconscious mind will try to protect us and hide it away in our psyche's archives. This can make us oversensitive or fearful and cause us to overreact to situations that we would otherwise not. When we overreact, we often behave irrationally.

Anxiety can also cause us to overgeneralize. Someone asks you what is wrong? And you reply, everything or everyone. This is overgeneralizing, and it's easy to do, especially when we feel overwhelmed. When this happens, the problem is often only one or a few specific things. Instead of overgeneralizing this way, we should clarify exactly what the issues are to separate and address them individually. If there are several issues, often in solving one, you solve many.

Top tip; When you feel overwhelmed, write down all of your issues or problems on a piece of paper. Look at them individually and ask yourself: what is my next best move given these circumstances?

When we suffer any fear-based thinking patterns, we need to be careful about using our inner dialogue. We need to practice and learn the art of rephrasing our self-talk. Using challenging phrases such as, I am depressed, I have anxiety, or am angry, is taking ownership of the issue. When we do this, we are reinforcing the belief, which makes us feel worse. By using a different narrative and rephrasing our self-talk, we will instantly feel better.

For example, Instead of saying I am depressed, you could say, Recently, I have been experiencing some depression. Instead of saying I have anxiety, you could say, I have been suffering anxiety for a while now. Instead of saying I am always angry, you could say, I've been feeling angry for a long time. *Notice how much softer and kinder this sounds.*

Top tip; Remember that you were not born with these feelings, which means they are temporary, and that all emotions are fleeting. When referring to yourself, never use strong negative words such as hate, disgust, or any language with harmful or derogatory connotations. Self-criticism should be said constructively, not destructively.

Practice: Using the following affirmations, repeat them repeatedly to yourself while you are confronting your anxiety: I fear nothing, I fear no one, and I can handle any situation.

Clearing Past Emotions

We all experience stressful, frightening, upsetting, and traumatic incidents during our upbringing and throughout life. Some of these incidents have a profound and long-lasting effect on our thinking and behavior. Whenever we experience what we feel to be a traumatic or a significant event, our subconscious mind processes and stores the memory. It then uses the memory of the experience to protect us by alerting us to any perceived or potential threats. When burdened with stored emotional memories/repression from the past, we are more likely to use avoidance and overreact in certain situations. It will also influence anxiety-related issues such as overthinking, over-analyzing, low moods, general fear, low confidence, irritability, frustration, habits, and addiction. All of which affect our levels of happiness. We all experience situations differently, and so traumatic and upsetting moments do not have to be from significant events. They can be caused by watching movies, embarrassing moments, or any perceived threat or danger.

Some of us have had more upsetting and traumatic moments than others, and some of us naturally handle our stored emotions better. Sometimes we can forget the events or the seriousness of how those events affected us at the time. They become tucked away in our minds' vault, and so it varies from person to person as to how much repression they are holding and as to how affected they are by it. But it is right to say that we are all keeping emotional memory/repression from past events. I call it emotional baggage because that, in layman's terms, is what it is.

Practice; Because we are reprogramming our minds for change, we must clear some of our repressed emotions. So let's offload some of our emotional baggage with your first hypnotherapy session, which is an audio download.

Now listen to **Hypnosis audio 001. Emotional Cleansing Repeat weekly for 4 weeks and then periodically.**

This will leave you feeling calm, relaxed, and generally lighter. Most importantly, you will have cleared some of those negative emotions you have been holding to, and is the perfect start for your journey or change *Complete this before moving to the next chapter.*

Chapter 4

The rhythm of Internal Love

Allow me to start with a question. How do you feel about yourself? Choose one of the following; love, like-dislike, or hate. In answering this question, you will gauge how far away you are from loving yourself. I'm not talking about selfish love, admiring how beautiful or talented you are. I'm talking about how you feel about yourself as a person—the relationship you have with your inner self.

I often hear people saying that they are looking for their soul mate, confidant, particular person, someone they can trust and be at one with, and someone who would never let them down. People worldwide are searching for this. Often they think they have found it in a relationship with someone they love, only to realize that they continue to feel insecure. Let me share some great news with you. It's been under your nose the whole time. Take a look in the mirror, and you will see it because it's YOU. When you develop an abundance of internal-love, you develop inner security, internal-trust, and internal-acceptance. And this eliminates feelings of insecurity and neediness of others. Without Internal-love, you will feel insecure and are likely to struggle throughout life. You will suffer self-doubt, low self-esteem, low confidence, and are likely to have inadequate coping mechanisms, suffering low moods. Many will experience depression, habits, and addiction. Those who are on the hate themselves scale may carry out acts of self-harm or even suicide, and in which case need urgent help.

When you meet someone to love and share your life with and feel secure, the love you feel will take you to another level of contentment and is the icing on the cake. Those that feel insecure and are in a relationship are likely to continue to feel insecure unless they have developed internal-love. Relying on others to make you feel secure will be temporary. Internal love = Security. We all have imperfection and things that we would like to change about ourselves, but this should not correlate to how we feel about ourselves. Each shortcoming that we have enables us to become better at something else. A blind man develops his sense of hearing or smell far beyond that of the person who has normal vision because he will gain a natural compensation for his lack of vision. And so we should not focus on our limitations but on improving the gifts and abilities that we have. We must accept our flaws and find ways to work around them, focusing on the things we can change and not the things we cannot.

In the past, I have been unkind, critical, and super harsh on myself. My inner-talk was awful, and I was always telling myself how rubbish I was at everything and how ugly I looked. I hated myself and, as a teenager, contemplated suicide. Many years later, I learned that the insecurity and anxiety I experienced affected how I felt about myself. I started to reframe how I talked to myself, developing positive affirmations, and re-evaluating my beliefs using evidence and facts only to identify the truth. Learning to like myself improved my confidence, and with liking myself, everything seemed a little easier. Then I started to think to myself, if liking myself makes me feel better and more confident, I wonder what loving myself could do? The trouble was that I incorrectly assumed it would mean that I would be seen as cocky or arrogant, which I have always believed to be an awful trait. Arrogance is a defense mechanism for insecurity and goes hand in hand with the constant need for approval, even if the arrogant person has achieved something extraordinary. Arrogant and cocky people are insecure.

As well as having to be the center of attention, arrogant people generally lack empathy. And this is how those who have developed internal- love differ from those that have not because those with internal-love are confident but humble, unlike arrogant individuals who are far from modest.

Several years later, during the time I had spent alone, studying new therapies, meditating for hours, and experimenting with affirmation, my feelings about myself shifted from like to love. I noticed how much more secure I had become.

The following year when I started working as a full-time hypnotherapist, I began to implement my newfound knowledge with clients. I found that internal-love wasn't just crucial for mental wellbeing but that it was critical. The change to those that learn to love themselves is extraordinary. It is the foundation of confidence, self-trust, self-acceptance, and self–value. Not only does it build inner security, but it also gifts inner peace and a psychological cushion that protects us in so many ways.

With self-love comes a great many things. We stop taking things so personally, and we stop over worrying about things that have not happened. We develop a high level of self-esteem, and with that comes a great deal of personal confidence. We learn to trust ourselves in all situations, and we do not allow others to control us, nor do we feel a need to control others. We know our worth, develop better relationships, become more independent, and are less fearful in all endeavors. Our chances of success in all we do increase significantly. When we think below par of ourselves, we will be plagued with self-doubt and think negatively in many situations, making us feel anxious and frustrated. When we suffer inner conflict, we make more wrong decisions and therefore hit more bumps in the road of life.

Your consciousness/soul/spirit is a unique present that is individual to you. Our bodies are vehicles for real experience.

Our spirit of mind is what makes us alive; otherwise, we would be zombies. No one on the planet has your spirit, and no two souls are the same. It is truly remarkable and something that we should acknowledge and praise. Suppose we love and are kind to our family members, close friends, and pets, and we respect our possessions, homes, and many other aspects of our lives. Why wouldn't we act in this way towards ourselves? When we do not respect or love our consciousness, we will have inner conflict and self-doubt, which stops us from feeling good about ourselves. In appreciating and respecting our consciousness, we are creating the act of self-love. We are saying that we accept who we are and that we value ourselves. Internal-love is about the connection we have to our spirit and mind. You are the person occupying your body.

So much of what we have learned has been imprinted into our belief system. We believe that the color blue is blue because this is what we have been led to believe. Many cultures and religions have different beliefs and values because they have had other learnings. A terrorist organization can radicalize a well-behaved, kind, and loving young person who has never put a foot wrong in life by changing a belief system. Imprinting, in this way, can create a mass murderer in a relatively short period, and that is a testament to the power of belief. Imagine then what is possible with a guided positive thought. When we dislike ourselves and do not trust our opinions or actions, we will not trust others. To correct this, we need to imprint new positive learnings to overwrite the negative. We do this by developing a relationship with ourselves.

Here are some facts

We are all worthy of love. If you can learn, you can make great things happen.

Your behavior is a choice, and your etiquette dictates the quality of your life.

Inner peace and happiness is an equal opportunity and a state of mind.

Success is achievable all in countries of democracy if you want it enough.

Self-Love practice.

For the next four-weeks, use this daily practice to develop a relationship with yourself.

Week 1-Morning routine.

Find a mirror, somewhere you have privacy, and look face on. Maintain eye contact with yourself throughout this practice.

At first, this may feel uncomfortable; you might feel silly, emotional, or even frightened, but don't worry. It's temporary and perfectly healthy.

Move close to the mirror. (Approximately 6-12inches) and look deep into your eyes.

Make an introduction to yourself; Hello (name) It's nice to meet you.

Ask, How you are feeling at this moment?

Respond to your inner dialogue/ self-talk. Suppose you are not feeling great, which is possible at this stage. Reassure yourself that everything will work out just fine and that those feelings are temporary. Unless you think you are feeling OK or good, in which case respond with gratitude. A simple Thank You will suffice.

Move back slightly from the mirror. (Approximately 12 -18 inches) and repeat the following affirmations ten times each, maintaining eye contact. Point your index finger toward yourself in the mirror as you speak.

You (use your name) fear nothing.

You (use your name) fear no one.

You (use your name) can handle any situation.

(Use your name) your best is always good enough.

Anything is possible (use your name.)

You (use your name) are a worthy person deserving of love, and every day you are going to learn to love yourself more.

Everyone deserves to value themselves and their feelings. You (use your name) are learning to appreciate yourself and your feelings more every day.

Changing your mindset and how you feel about yourself (use your name) is only new learning.

Daily routine.

Repeat these affirmations ten times each, every 30 minutes out loud. If that's not possible in your mind, out loud is preferable.

I fear nothing

I fear no one

I can handle any situation.

My best is always good enough.

Anything is possible.

Evening routine.

Find a mirror again, where you have privacy, and look face on. Maintain eye contact with yourself throughout this whole experience.

Now get close to the mirror (Approximately 6-12inches) and look deep into your eyes.

Start with gratitude. Thank you for the day today and the new learnings I have experienced.

Move back slightly from the mirror. (Approximately 12-18 inches) and repeat the following affirmations ten times each.

You (use your name) have as much right as anyone to inner peace and calm.

You (use your name) fear nothing.

You (use your name) fear no one.

You (use your name) can handle any situation.

You (use your name) are a worthy person deserved of love, and every day you are learning to love and trust yourself more and more.

Anything is possible (use your name)

Everyone deserves to value themselves, and their feelings, and (use your name) are learning to appreciate yourself and your feelings more and more every day.

You (use your name) deserve the best.

Week 2 - Morning routine.

Back to the mirror in private, and look face on. Maintain eye contact with yourself throughout this practice.

Looking into your eyes close to the mirror as you did last week. (Approximately 6-12inches away)

Make your morning introduction; Good morning (use your name); how are you feeling today?

Respond to your inner dialogue/ self-talk. If you think you are feeling OK or good, respond by saying I am doing much better; thank you. If you are not feeling great, reassure yourself that everything will work out just fine because the feeling is temporary.

Move back slightly from the mirror, so you are (Approximately 12 -18 inches away) and repeat the following affirmations five times each, maintaining eye contact. Point your index finger towards yourself in the mirror as you speak.

You (use your name) fear nothing.

You (use your name) fear no one.

You (use your name) can handle any situation.

You (use your name) are very worthy, and I love you more and more every day.

You (use your name) deserve great things in your life.

You (use your name) are amazing.

Anything is possible (use your name.)

Day routine.

Take a moment to think about the things you are good at or what other people think you are good at. List those qualities and attributes onto a piece of paper and read them out to yourself. Add to them each time you think of something new or when someone pays you a compliment.

For example, I am good at, I am kind, I am caring, I am a good friend, partner, spouse, son, daughter, brother, sister, parent. I am good at my job, I am reliable, I am hardworking, I am honest, I am loyal, I am thoughtful, etc.

Repeat these below affirmations ten times each, every 30 minutes out loud, or if that's not possible, in your mind, out loud is preferable.

I fear nothing or no one.

I can handle any situation.

I am worthy of self-love.

I am amazing.

My best is always good enough.

I deserve great things.

Anything is possible.

Evening routine.

Find a mirror again, in privacy, look face on. Maintain eye contact throughout this practice.

Now get close to the mirror. (Approximately 6-12inches) and focus on your eyes.

Start with gratitude. Thank you for the day and all the positive feelings you have given me.

Move back slightly from the mirror. (Approximately 12-18 inches) and repeat the following affirmations five times each.

You (use your name) are feeling better and better every day.

You (use your name) are feeling more and more confident every day.

You (use your name) are worthy, and I love you.

You are an amazing person. (use your name)

Anything is possible (use your name)

You (use your name) deserve the best.

Week 3 - Morning routine.

Back to the mirror in private, and standing face on. Maintain eye contact with yourself throughout this practice.

Looking into your eyes close to the mirror. (Approximately 12-18 inches)

Make your morning introduction; Good morning, you amazing, worthy person.

Respond to your inner dialogue/ self-talk, and if you think you are feeling OK or good, respond by saying I am doing great, thank you. Every day, I'm feeling better and better. If you are not feeling great, say, I am having an off day, but it's temporary, and I know that things will improve.

Repeat the following affirmations ten times each, maintaining eye contact.

Point your index finger toward yourself in the mirror as you speak.

You (use your name) are becoming more and more confident.

You (use your name) love yourself more and more every day.

You (use your name) fear nothing and no one.

You (use your name) can manage any situation.

You (use your name) are moving towards the life you deserve.

You (use your name) are proud of the person you are becoming.

You (use your name) deserve great things to happen.

Thank you for this amazing journey of discovery and change.

Anything is possible. (use your name)

Day routine.

Read out the list of your qualities and attributes and continue to add new ones as and when you think of them.

Repeat these affirmations ten times each, every 30 minutes out loud, or if that's not possible in your mind. Out loud is preferable.

I fear nothing or no one.

I can handle any situation.

I am an amazing person.

I love myself more and more.

I am confident.

My best is always good enough.

I deserve an amazing life.

Anything is possible

Evening routine.

Back to the mirror and look face on. (Approximately 12-18 inches) Maintain eye contact throughout this practice.

Start with gratitude; Thank you for today's experiences and learnings.

Repeat the following affirmations ten times each.

You (use your name) are feeling better and better every day.

You (use your name) are feeling more and more confident every day.

You (use your name) are so worthy of so many amazing things.

I love and admire you. (use your name)

You (use your name) deserve the best.

Week 4 - Morning routine.

Back to the mirror and looking face on. (Approximately 12-18 inches) Maintain eye contact throughout this practice.

Make your morning introduction; Good morning (use your name), you worthy person. I love and appreciate you. Thank you, the universe, for all the great things I have in my life, (Think of the things that you love and enjoy and say them out loud.) How are you this morning? I wonder what amazing things might happen today?

Repeat the following affirmations ten times each, maintaining eye contact.

Point your index finger toward yourself in the mirror as you speak.

You (use your name) love yourself because you (use your name) are amazing.

You (use your name) fear nothing or no one, and you can handle any situation.

You (use your name) have so much to look forward to.

You (use your name) are confident, secure, and capable of achieving anything you put your mind to.

Day routine.

Rewrite your list of qualities and attributes. Read them out loud.

Repeat these affirmations ten times each, every 30 minutes out loud, or if that's not possible in your mind. Out loud is preferable.

I fear nothing or no one.

I can handle any situation.

I am so amazing.

I love myself very much.

I am confident and strong.

My best is always good enough.

I can achieve anything I put my mind to.

Evening routine.

Find a mirror again, where you have privacy, looking face on. (Approximately 12-18 inches) Maintain eye contact.

Start with gratitude and say; Thank you for today's experiences and learnings. Thank you in advance for all the amazing things that are going to happen in my life.

Repeat the following affirmations five times each.

Life is getting better and better every day. (use your name)

I love and accept everything about you (use your name), even my flaws.

Nothing phases you (use your name) because you are mentally healthy, strong, confident, and capable of making anything happen.

Your best is always good enough. (use your name)

Anything is possible. (use your name)

You (use your name) deserve the best.

Once you have completed this four-week practice, you can start to have open, honest, and curious chats with yourself. You can offload your worries and frustrations by talking them through with yourself. You can ask questions or deliberate using self-talk about any decisions or issues you may have. You will get to know yourself better and better with this practice, and in doing this, you will learn to become your own counselor. Create new affirmations as necessary and use them as and when you need to. Commitment to affirmation brings real power and something that I would encourage you to use ongoing. There is no one to judge you, no rules or laws to obey. Your mind is exclusively yours, and for you alone, so say things as they are and project your true feelings and thoughts. Be yourself and not what others want you to be, maintaining integrity and using a moral compass. Listen to your thoughts as you ask questions, and you can even take notes if it helps. Your subconscious mind doesn't lie to you. You can be that person we spoke about earlier, your new best friend, companion, and confidant. The person who is always there for you to trust, love, and ask for advice. You will feel calmer and more confident. And while there will always be room for further improvement, you will become mentally more robust, more confident, and more in touch with who you. There is no limit. Each of us is a unique and special being that deserves to be secure and happy.

Practice; Confidence and self-esteem booster. Choose a song that is uplifting and motivates you positively. Play this song or piece of music inside your head, or you can hum or whistle. Now set your body posture by pulling your shoulders back, holding your head up high. Visualize a bubble around you, and this is your space. Start walking, and as you walk, tune in to your legs and feet, noticing each stride, and as you do this, visualize yourself connecting to the earth with every step you take. Imagine owning the ground underneath your feet as you walk. Repeat to yourself (mine, mine) with every step you take and do this for 5-10 minutes daily for a few weeks. You will notice how self-assured and confident this makes you feel, building your self-esteem. Possession is 9/10ths of the law

Chapter 5

Combatting Negativity

Managing Negativity

Negativity is a life-limiting disease of the mind. Negative thinkers find reasons for not enjoying life; they moan, complain, and blame. They see the dark side of every situation because that is where their minds are focused. In other words, they are looking for it. The sad thing is that they are not living life to its full potential and, as a result, feel dissatisfied and resentful. Misery loves company and alike attracts alike, so negative people tend to hang out with others that are also negative. Suppose you are a positive person trapped in either a work or home environment of negativity. In that case, it can be very challenging to stay positive, and you will have to work pretty hard to stop others from dampening your sparkles. Then there is also the negative person who doesn't acknowledge the negativity he or she is breeding, claiming that he or she is a realist. This type of person often goes against what has been said in a contrary manner. They are the ones who will tell you that you cant achieve things and will give a reason, somehow always managing to find a pinch point for an argument.

The projection of negative energy is asking for negative experiences in return. I have been trying to think of something positive to say about being negative, and there are only two things that I can come up with. The first is that a little pessimism can be helpful in matters of safety and caution. The optimist invented the aircraft, and the pessimist invented the parachute. Still, even then, it's a positive spin on a potentially harmful situation. Secondly, we can use it to find the strength to drive us positively forward. And this can make you more determined, allowing you to prove those doom merchants wrong.

I've been browbeaten, ridiculed, and reminded of my failings and mistakes for the whole of my life. Even today, my future goals and aspirations come under criticism. Somehow I have managed to find a way to flip this into a fierce determination to prove them wrong. I start by becoming annoyed about the negativity directed at me.

When I become annoyed, I become determined to show others what I can do. When I become determined, I become an unstoppable force.

And when I become an unstoppable force, I make things happen.

When we have a reason to achieve, we stay more focused and driven. My way of becoming motivated may seem a little extreme for some, but it works for me. You can find a focus that works for you. It doesn't matter how you find your mojo as long as you do and that you do it with integrity, not harming anyone in the process. You will encounter setbacks, and you are likely to be met with further criticism and resistance, but that's when you need to show your metal and self-believe. Negativity is a choice you should never make. Be that Roman Gladiator and make it happen.

Criticizing and Control

Donna was having an affair with a Turkish man called Ender that owned the local takeaway. One day her mother in law, while in the area, made a surprise visit and caught Ender and Donna busy sharing some Turkish delight in the kitchen. Which wouldn't have been a problem, except that they were hand-feeding each other at the time.

Things got messy, and a week later, Martin was asked to leave the house. Martin took the relationship with the kebab shop owner really hard, especially as he'd been vegetarian for the past 15 years. He was stressed beyond belief and suffered poor sleep patterns, sleeping like a one-eyed sailor on a night watch.

Martin couldn't handle the ongoing situation at home with Donna, who openly continued her relationship with Ender. Martin had reluctantly moved into a scruffy one-bedroom flat, which was all he could afford. At the same time, Donna and the children continued to live in the comfort of their former four-bedroom detached marital home.

Martin believed that he had done nothing wrong, as it was his ex-wife that had an affair and broke up the family. She continued to push him financially, using the children as weapons.

Three years had passed by, and he became a former shadow of the man he was, very thin and gaunt. He was full of anger, turning to alcohol for comfort. His good friend and work colleague became concerned about him and talked him into seeing a therapist. After listening to his story, the therapist pointed out how stuck Martin had become. That he had allowed his ex-wife to continue to control his emotions, affecting his happiness and wellbeing. And that the suppression of his feelings was causing him to continue feeling angry and depressed.

Martin said that he had punched holes in the doors in his flat due to his anger. The therapist reminded him that it had been over three years since the split. He told Martin that he should bear some of the responsibility for the breakup. And then asked him what role in the break up he had played; even if it was merely marrying the wrong person, you played a part, "he said." He explained that Martin needed to accept and work with what has happened to regain control of his life.

Donna was given legal custody of the children, and Martin always felt at the mercy of her decisions until his son came of age, reminding Martin that this was a temporary situation. He stood to receive 50% of the house's equity when the children were of age. That it was, effectively, a saving scheme for him, as well as stability for his children. The therapist then asked him, "Why do you accept defeat and continue to feel sorry for yourself because you are playing into Donna's hands. The way I see it is you are giving her the satisfaction and control she craves, which means that she is winning over and over"? Do you know that you can stop this right now if you want and turn this situation around"?

Martin took this on board, and as his mindset started to change, he began to see things from a different perspective.

After a few days of pondering and some hypnosis from the therapist, the old Martin came back, full of vitality.

His problem was he still had to tackle Donna's criticizing and controlling aspect, so he immediately stopped drinking and joined the gym.

Donna and Ender were now jointly running the takeaway. Martin was to drop his sons at the takeaway after a visit when Martin noticed that the shop next door was empty. He thought about it for a while and contacted the landlord, agreeing to rent the shop. He then took a loan from the equity in his former home and signed the lease.

As soon as the legal transaction was done, he put a new sign up, naming his store Turkish Delight. He placed a temporary banner in the window, which read; Cheap Donna kebab & The Turkish Off-Ender coming soon. Hot broth and spicy sauce for afternoon delight available here. This started to gain a lot of publicity in the neighborhood.

Donna saw Martin in the shop and approached him with venom, yelling.

"What the hell do you think you are doing"?

"As you can see, I am now the owner of this shop Donna. I'm thinking of renting it out to Larry. He wants it as a reptile store; the trouble is they are very stinky, especially the fish bate he sells."

Donna said, "So gruesome can you afford this shop."

Martin replied, "It's none of your business Donna, but I should let you know that I've used our house as security on this lease. I am hoping that I won't have any problems with you and Ender as I wouldn't want to have any legal issues with yours and the children's home."

With a smug look, he bid her a good day and skipped off down the street.

Donna was seething, and Ender increasingly concerned about the effect of this on his business, not to mention the embarrassment of the sign in the window.

This continued for a few days when a local journalist that happened to know Martin was found snooping around. In her usual criticolling manner, Donna approached Martin and told him to remove the sign from the window. Martin said no and offered to rent her and Ender the unit on a monthly lease, which she vehemently refused.

A few hours later, Ender approached him. They agreed to terms on the unit's rental to arrange that Ender could relet the premises to someone else on a monthly rent. And so they did the deal. At that moment, Martin took back control. No longer was he going to be controlled or criticized (criticolling) by Donna or Ender.

Martin asked if he could take his son's on vacation the following week, to which, of course, she had no problem. He took them for a two-week break to Istanbul. It really was a Turkish delight to be sat down eating a Donna Kebab with his two son's and never again would he need to have to worry about being criticized or controlled by Donna again.

Those in control of their lives are conducting their own orchestra and choosing the music they want to listen to. Allowing anyone to control you is not a good thing, and even worse if it's someone who doesn't have your back and is determined to ruin you. Living in a swell of self-pity and negativity can block us from attracting the positive things we want. Remember that the laws of the universe respond according to what you put out. There will always be certain circumstances and situations that we cannot control and the conditions we have to accept. But we can forever control how we perceive or interoperate what others say or do. We can especially control how we react.

Criticolling

I have come across many people who constantly criticize and control others. Noticing how prevalent this issue is, I started to think that it should be recognized in its own right as a mental health issue. With that belief, I created a word that encompasses the combined act of criticizing and control, which I have named criticolling, and has now been, published in the urban dictionary, with the following definition.

To use criticism and control together towards another person is criticolling. Pronounced, CRITIKOWLING

Those that criticize and control others are criticoller's.

Pronounced, CRITIKOWLER'S

Example: John is criticolling towards his wife and children, and therefore, he is a criticoller.

There are two types of criticoller's as explained below. One of which is more severe than the other.

Type 1 criticollers use criticism and control towards others without considering the other person's feelings. These dominant individuals will demand authority, often using an aggressive demeanor or using strong language. They will insist on things being on their terms and being done their way because it is all about them. They lack empathy, care, or compassion for another's needs. Often brow beaters or bullies, these individuals rarely pay compliments, offer help or encourage others positively unless there is something in it for them.

They consider their own needs only and not the needs of others. They will always be right about everything and often contrary, causing the sufferer to feel inferior and incompetent in making their own decisions. They will struggle in relationships and, if not alone, will choose an insecure and submissive partner. Type 1 criticoller's will often use belittling and put down comments such as; What the hell wrong is with you? Are you that useless? Can't you even do that simple task? This type of behavior depletes confidence and lowers self-esteem in others, and is emotionally abusive behavior.

Type 2 criticollers are less aggressive in their approach but do have love and empathy for the person they are criticolling. Thus, they consider themselves kind, believing that they are helping the other person, and acting in their best interest. Often they think the other person to be incompetent in their abilities and that they are always right with their advice. Unlike type 1, they do not use harsh language to manipulate because they care for the person they are criticolling.

When we criticize and control others, it stops that person from learning for themselves, and developing confidence or self-esteem. It also prevents them from developing problem-solving skills and causes them to depend on others, become unsure of their abilities, and be plagued with self-doubt. This negativity is particularly damaging to a child's development. Children raised in environments drenched in criticism and control often develop anxiety or frustration issues.

I hope that people share this and create awareness of this harmful and wrongful way of treating others. With knowledge, it is possible to break the pattern. Those that want to control others are unable to control themselves. They are unaware of their destructive behavior, which could easily be changed. Of course, there will always be a need for constructive criticism, discipline, and guidance in others. Still, it needs to be implemented in a nurturing way to bring out the best, not a criticizing way.

Celebrities, pop stars, politicians, and others in the public eye have to deal with criticism every day. The best way for them they cope with this is by not allowing themselves to take things personally.

No one has the right to criticize and control anyone. Expecting others to be like you is both unrealistic and unreasonable. Real power is not in controlling others; it is in controlling yourself. Each of us has the absolute right to live our life on our terms, make our own decisions, and live the way we choose, as long as it's ethical, legal, and not hurting anyone. By that, I don't mean hurting anyone else's feelings. We all have limited time on this earth, and we should be making our own choices without the fear of being put down, ridiculed, or controlled.

Transference

Whenever we meet someone, we give and receive what is known as Transference. It is a two-way subliminal projection of energy that provides us with a feeling about the other person. When we meet someone we have never met before, we make our minds up as to whether we like, or dislike them. We do this automatically, even without knowing anything about them or anything about their lives. There are many reasons why someone can take an instinctive dislike to us. Perhaps something about you reminds them of someone they dislike or a trait that they despise. Maybe they are envious of you somehow. Those who dislike themselves will invariably find reasons not to like others. When we take a natural like to someone, it will be because that other person has qualities we admire, things in common with us, or somehow we can relate to them. Those who love themselves will not dislike others without good reason. If you are polite and friendly, you will never need to take a situation like this personally from someone you do not know.

Handling Loss

Loss is the blight of human experience and always unpleasant. It is the one thing we all dread, and none of us can avoid it. There are many different types of loss, and the pain of loss varies depending on what the loss is. A lost opportunity is frustrating, but there will always be more opportunities. Financial loss is excruciating but replaceable with hard work. Losing material possessions can be extremely upsetting, but again they are usually replaceable in some way unless there is sentimental attachment. The good news about these losses, is that they are not life-threatening. If we lose our health, we do have a big problem, but we can do something about it. We can accept the situation and fight to recover, giving us hope. Still, as with all loss, acceptance is the first step to recovery. Once we accept what has happened, we can move forward. If we break up with a partner, there will be someone else out there for us, and when we find one, it is likely to be a better relationship than the one that ended. Often when we replace something that we have lost, it turns out to be better.

Those separated or divorced that feel they lost their children; know that they will always be yours. Regardless of the situation or the distance, no one can ever take that away from you. As long as you continue to work at it, you will always have that relationship even from afar. No one can take your memories away.

The worst type of loss is to lose someone we love through bereavement because it's so final, and when this occurs, it empties our souls, robs our happiness, and brings lasting change. We cannot bring a person back, but we can keep the memory of that person alive. By bringing the memory into the present, we can stay close and connected to that person, and in doing so, honor their life. One of the best ways to do this is to create a memory flower garden. You can add a plaque or keepsake of that person and make a beautiful spiritual connection between the flower garden and the person you lost. It is there for you to tender, smell, enjoy, reminisce, and even chat too. Not only is this a memory garden, but also therapy, bringing positive energy and comfort into your life daily. If you do not have a garden, you can instead use plants in a pot. Or perhaps purchase an ornament, a piece of art or furniture, so that you, too, can honor that person's life and maintain a spiritual connection and a positive memory. If you have an inheritance, then invest it into something that will be a lasting memory.

Appearance and Standards

Society places a great deal of expectation on us all. So whether we like it or not, we live in a world where our image and the way we come across to others matter hugely. Others judge us on how we present and express ourselves; in dress, work, speech, appearance, attitude, wit, charm, integrity, empathy, and kindness. These traits also impact what we think about others, too: many people will judge you on a first impression. Keeping yourself well-groomed and presented, coming across polite, respectful, and grateful to others will enhance your overall appearance and attractiveness too. We rely on others for many things, so how we are perceived correlates to our quality of life.

Your home is your base camp and where you spend most of your time, so living in an organized, clean, clutter-free environment makes you feel more in control and happy. It says a lot about you to others too. Investing in your home is investing in yourself, and investing in yourself is the best investment you can ever make.

Thinking before Responding

Many people use terms such as; I call a spade a spade, or I am not shy in coming forward; to justify their outspokenness. This means that they struggle to think before speaking or reacting and fail to consider the other person's feelings or simply lack respect. This inability to control one's words or actions will make you unpopular and bring many unexpected problems throughout life. It really is poor etiquette.

Top tip; Those they act in this way can improve their self-control by being more concerned about the other person and how your actions and words affect their feelings. Thinking through what you are going to say and practicing better delivery will help. Speak kindly, and be respectful always. You can soften your vocabulary with add-ons either before you talk or after. For example, please don't take this the wrong way, but... Or, I mean this respectfully, Or I apologize if I come over harsh. - Something that cushions your wording. You can say anything if you say it nicely, and the more you practice this, the better you will become. Also, give yourself some time before speaking or responding so that you do not knee jerk react.

Flexibility of Thinking

George and Elsie have been married for over 30 years. George, a retired school - teacher, and Elsie worked in a local accountants office. They have always been a very social couple, enjoying drinks during the evenings. Since retirement, George started slipping into the habit of going to the local pub for a couple of drinks on his way home from his daily trip to the stores. Then once home, he would crack open a bottle of wine for what he calls his pre-evening lubricator, claiming that shopping makes him thirsty.

Elsie had become increasingly frustrated, accusing George of being intoxicated by the time she gets home from work, which had led to several fights. Of course, George denies being drunk when she gets home, argues that he is retired, has worked, and has provided for the family for over 30 years. He also points out that they have no financial problems and works through choice, not need. He further reminded her that he does all the house chores and the daily grocery run.

Elsie could be pretty brutal at times and always wanting things her way too. She started by telling George that he doesn't spend any quality time with her. Since retirement, she said, "He has been drinking like a delinquent Irish priest at an all-inclusive resort." She further reminded him that retirement was not a vacation. Then she went on to say that falling asleep after dinner and snoring like a pig in the armchair at full volume is unacceptable. Especially when she can't even hear her TV programs.

It's not often that George gets that type of praise from his wife and, as always, promptly thanked her for the compliments. Still, it did resonate with him. Unsure of what to do, he thought about getting some advice. For entertainment, he chose to confide in a local barmaid called Julie down at "The Hatch." Julie wasn't exactly wife or Mother of the year with four previous husbands and three dysfunctional children. She said, "Husband number four was fortunately still in prison after forcing one of her sons to help him hold up the local post office. She claimed that she would kill him as soon as he gets out, and her ex-husband wasn't exactly in her good books either.

After explaining the situation, George offered fifty dollars if she could think of a solution to his problem. She pondered for about a nanosecond and replied, "Sure, it's easy; just dump her, and then you can come to the pub every day. In fact, you can do whatever you want every day." Then she went on to say how she remembered divorcing one of her ex-husbands because she sent "the lazy fat git" to the shop for some slim fast milk. Instead, he went to the McDonalds drive-through and bought himself a cheeseburger. "It was all the money we had," She exclaimed.

George sarcastically mentioned to her how good it was that she didn't hold grudges. He then advised her that she probably shouldn't go into marriage counseling as a career, proceeding to explain the importance of compromise. A word he thought she would be unlikely to be able to spell, let alone understand. As he left, Julie asked about the fifty dollars that he offered, to which he flippantly replied, "After that conversation, Julie, I think I should be charging you."

The next day he contacted a friend and colleague. Joe was the former union representative, at the school teachers association. George remembered that he was also someone who could complete a Rubik's cube and so thought he might help him solve his issue.

George called him up and explaining his situation. Joe suggested that George went to the store a little later in the day and missed out on the pub. Then he would arrive home around the same time as Elsie so that his first glass of wine is with her. "Then," he said, "She will have no reason to be upset with you because you will be sober. You won't fall asleep too early, and you can enjoy a few glasses of wine in the evening with a happy wife. All you have to do is be flexible in your thinking."

"That's a great idea, but I really like going to the pub."

"Well, I guess you can't have everything, George."

"Thank you, Joe I will implement this straight away" And the problem with Elsie was solved as quickly as that, but George still wanted to go to the pub. He missed the banter with Julie and chatting with the locals. George started to ponder on the flexibility of thinking notion and hatched a plan. Knowing that Elsie would always go to bed around 9.30pm and the pub was only a few minute's walks away, he figured that he could go for a pint after she had gone to bed. To execute his plan effectively, George went to bed with Elsie at 9.30pm on the first night, overly enhancing his snoring, deliberately to keep her awake. The next evening George asked Elsie if she would mind him going to the pub when she goes to bed, knowing that Elsie would welcome the peace from his snoring. From that moment, George was able to go to the pub every evening during the week after Elsie had gone to bed.

The first night he arrived at the pub, full of beans, well, wine actually. However, he did have beans for dinner. In he walked, and Julie was standing behind the bar, looking as happy as ever. "Fancy seeing you here, has she kicked you out,' she quipped"?

With a smile wider than Dolly Parton's bra, and called out, "A pint of your finest, please, my love?

It's worked out beautifully. My Elsie wants things her own way and tries to make my life difficult, but I have sorted her right out. I wake up at leisure in the mornings, take a walk to the store in the afternoons, have a few glasses of wine over dinner, come to the pub when the wife is in bed, without restriction, by the way.

I can enjoy a bit of banter and chat with a few locals. Then I go home, fall into bed, and snore until my heart is content. Yes, I am on vacation, permanent vacation, actually.

There is always another way around things, Julie. It's all about the flexibility of thinking. And just in case my snoring wakes her, I have left a Rubik's cube on the side table to encourage her to develop some thinking flexibility herself. She's an accountant, so she can always count on me to find a solution.

Whenever you experience a problem that you are struggling to resolve in virtually every situation, there are always more and better choices. When we open our minds and use the flexibility of thought, our options dramatically increase, and more solutions appear. There are always different options. People who are too rigid in their thoughts and unprepared to compromise are unlikely to gain the best outcome. Rigorous thinking without compromise leads to resentment, arguments, frustration, and inevitable loss.

The best outcome will always be the one that works for all and not just for one or few. Those who find it difficult to accept an outcome because it's not their preferred choice must realize the importance of choosing the best result given the circumstances and situation. There is always middle ground if you look hard enough.

Practice; Breathing meditation

We are encouraged to keep our bodies healthy by exercising, and rightly so, but what about our minds? Our minds also need something to keep them healthier too. Our brains are kept very busy and are continually working; even when we sleep, our brains stay active, so what can we do about this.

Meditation is scientifically proven to change our brains' structure. It develops emotional wellness, helps control stress and anxiety, enhances clarity of thought, better sleep, and many other cognitive benefits.

Meditations do not have set times, but around 20 minutes is ideal.

For this breathing meditation practice, ensure you sit comfortably upright, loosen any tight clothing, and remove any distractions.

You can cross your legs, but it is not essential; what is important is that you are comfortable, upright, and in a quiet environment.

Close your eyes, and take some nice deep breaths, and permit yourself to relax by saying, I allow myself to relax. Repeat this five times.

It takes practice so don't worry if you find it difficult or fall asleep; the important thing is to do it regularly. You will be amazed at the results.

Now it's time to listen to the **Hypnosis audio 002 –GUIDED MEDITATION** from the download list.

Chapter 6

Knowing how you Roll

To know yourself

Graham suffered from anxiety and had a bit of a twitch, which he had from childhood. It was a sort of a shoulder jerk with a shake of the head. He was geeky, sensitive, intelligent, and very likable. His parents were fabulous people. However, his father was a little eccentric and very superstitious. He was obsessive about rubbing the belly of a fat wooden Buddha they kept on the mantle. He believed it to bring him good luck.

When Graham reached adolescence, he became very interested in bird watching. He was given a pair of binoculars and a camera for his birthday, and he was set. His favorite was tits, all types, shapes, and sizes. He loved to watch and photograph them going about their business, particularly in the summer. He would climb trees wearing camouflage so he could shoot without being seen. He became so excited to see tits coming out of their nest that it caused his twitch to accelerate. His shoulder and head would start jerking like a dysfunctional flipper on a pinball machine, and on one occasion, it had caused him to fall out of the tree. Fortunately, he was only shaken up but very embarrassed. His neighbor was putting out the washing at the time.

Graham aspired for success from a very young age, and it wasn't going to be as a surgeon. He was primed and nurtured by his parents for a prestigious career. After university, Graham found a position within a corporate company that had plenty of potential for promotion. Still, it meant that he would have to start in the mailroom, and he slowly climbed the corporate ladder.

Some ten years later, his dream had finally come true, and he became the company's CEO. His parents and all those who knew him were so proud of his achievement. A few weeks after his promotion, he learned that he had to make 150 employees redundant. He was already under extreme pressure due to hitting targets and was fire fighting all kinds of issues daily. It was a different job to what he had been used to, and the responsibility weighed heavily upon his shoulders. It took a massive toll on him, and he became more and more stressed. A work colleague who was his friend began crying in front of him about losing his livelihood. It became too much, working long hours, not sleeping at night, and at the age of just 42, he suffered a heart attack while also on the verge of a nervous breakdown.

After surgery and convalescing for several weeks, he became fearful of returning to work and engaged in therapy. During this time, he reflected and learned that he wasn't cut out for his job role, even though it was something he had worked towards since he was a child. His personality type and default nature were wrong for such a commanding position. It wasn't for him, and he realized that he needed to be much more robust and less sensitive to manage a job like that -he was too friendly and soft natured for his career. He had wasted many years working towards something he wasn't suited to. The pressure was way too much for such a sensitive soul. The problem was that he had spent all those years learning his craft but didn't know about himself. His focus had been on attaining the highest position he could. Wanting to impress his parents and make money instead of considering what career would best suit him and make him happy.

Accepting this and recognizing the importance of a less stressed life, the therapist encouraged him to find something he would be more suited to and passionate about. He said he was passionate about birds and happiest working back working in the mailroom all those years ago.

A few months later, I caught up with him. He told me that he was working for the postal service as a mailman and really enjoyed having no pressure. He said, “My previous job sent me a bit cuckoo, and now I prefer to work with letters on my shoulder rather than after my name. I get to spot the odd tit on my round, and there are plenty of other birds to watch too. I tweet my findings to fellow twitchers, so yeah, life is good." Asking how his father felt about his change, he said, Dad feels it was his fault things went wrong, as he had been rubbing the Buddha in the wrong place for the past 15 years, which he feels embarrassed about. He said, "As luck would have it, a friend of your Mothers offered me a pair of great tits to bring me good luck. Naturally, I accepted, and since I, too, have developed a bit of a twitch. I guess I have always been a twitcher on the quiet son.

Self-wisdom is a great tool to have; the more you self explore, the better you will know yourself, and the more self-wisdom you will accrue. Self-study allows us to make better, more informed choices.

Periodically in life, we make big decisions, and these decisions can significantly impact our lives. Whenever we make a life decision, we need to thoroughly consider our capabilities and limitations too, but positively using self-honesty and facts. Working towards anything for an extended period, only to find that it doesn't work for you when you get there is a significant backward step. Forewarned is forearmed, hence the importance of knowing yourself. Knowing what you can handle and what you cannot is vital. We need to be congruent with our values and marry up our skills to our career and personal choices. We should note the sacrifice or compromise that a long–term commitment might mean, to see things for what they are.

Non-Judgmental

It is a challenging thing to be non-judgmental, and so the best way to practice this is to know that you are not better than anyone else and that know no one is better than you. We may be better practiced at specific tasks or have more ability, but this does not make us better or more superior to anyone else. We all deserve equality regardless of talents, abilities, success, appearance, wealth, fame, sexuality, race, or ethnicity.

When we recognize that every story has a story, we learn that we rarely, if ever, know all the facts of a situation. Therefore, we are often basing our judgment on limited knowledge. It's easy to think that you know what is best for others. Still, often we do not because we do not know the full circumstances, thoughts, biases, beliefs, and knowledge that person has. If a person disagrees with us, it is their purgative because we are all entitled to their view. We have no right to judge others for their decisions as long as they are mot immoral or harmful. Each of us can choose our preferences, make our own decisions, and live a life of authenticity and be true to our feelings and desires. We must accept that our views may not be right for the other person.

Taking yourself too Seriously

Here's a silly poem.

When walking down the street, I smile at everyone.

To make others feel positive and to have a little fun.

I smiled at a girl who was looking rather sad.

Her boyfriend didn't like it, and it made him pretty mad.

He shouted out to me, stop smiling at my chick

I'm only preaching happiness, you insecure git.

I smile at the elderly, and I smile at the young.

Sometimes I get excited and wiggle out my tongue.

I am only being friendly, as I jovially blow a kiss.

I want to make people smile, so how can I resist

Some they smile back, and some gasp in disbelief.

Especially those that notice that I don't have any teeth

What is most important is the way we feel within

So whenever you see another person, give a great big cheeky grin.

Taking yourself too seriously is a problem for anyone who wants to live happily and have minimum stress. Of course there are times when it is appropriate to be serious and times when it is not, and it is essential to know the difference. Often we can become uptight and rigid about things that do not matter that much. So what, if we spill a cup of coffee, clean it up and move on, or if we leave the washing out and it rains, or someone jumps the queue. Too often, we are stressed about unnecessary things. Ask yourself, is this the end of the world? Will this matter tomorrow? Next week? Next year?

Stress is a killer, causing us disease and illness. People are making themselves ill by being constantly stressed out over trivial matters. Living a life where everything matters will make things more likely to go wrong. Everyone has pressure to contend with, but how much it affects us is dependent on how we interpret it. We usually get a better outcome when we are less worried about the situation. Eric Byrne, the Canadian psychologist, and writer of Transactional Analysis, explained that we are all made up of three parts, Parent, Adult, and Child. Most people believe that our age dictates when we should be a parent, child, or an adult, but this is not true, as we are all of these things at certain times, for the duration of our lives. Regardless of age and appropriate to one's circumstance, there is always time to be playful like a child, sensible like an adult, and responsible like a parent. Having fun and being playful is essential for all of us. It fills us with joy and stimulates our brains, releasing dopamine, oxytocin, serotonin, and endorphins, making us feel good.

Top tip; A sense of humor is one of the most fantastic attractions in a human being. People gravitate toward those that can make others laugh and those who laugh a lot, so laugh often, and you will be considered a great person to be around and make many friends. Chuckling brings so much joy and has therapeutic benefits. There are many ways to do this, such as watching a comedy, telling a joke, pulling a funny face, talking in a silly voice, or saying whatever comes into your mind. Anything that promotes humor is positive and not only can make your day, but someone else's too.

Laughter is contagious, and life is short, so take yourself less seriously, and practice having fun. You will be amazed at how relaxed and happy you and others around you will feel.

Loneliness & Friendship

Those who feel alone, lack friends, or think that no one cares about them have likely failed to invest positively in others. Or they have not treated others with enough kindness or respect. If you are not investing positively in others, you cannot expect a positive return from others.

All of us have a built-in default setting of "what's in it for me." And we all have to reciprocate or give to get, whether it's love, kindness, support, humor, entertainment, good conversation, or something else that the other person wants or needs. If we stop giving, then we stop receiving. Even parents expect something in return from their children, even if it is only good manners or appreciation.

Those who are fortunate enough to have many friends hugely benefit from the diversity of different characters in their life because they gain something different from each person. Perhaps one of your friends is a good laugh but a blabbermouth, you can have a fabulous time with that person, but you may have to be careful what you say. Another may be very supportive and comforting, but no fun to go out with, etc. And this is why having a mixture of friends can be such a great thing. Those that have the right circle of friends live happier and more joyful lives. We do not need many friends, but we do need at least one good one.

People like to be around those that they have something in common with. Honesty and sincerity will hold long-term friendships and relationships because of the developed and earned trust. Trust is critical for stable relationships and friendships. If you are considered untrustworthy, you will find good people distancing themselves from you.

Loneliness is a psychological state of withdrawal from others. We are born apart, and we die alone. Nevertheless, in general, we are social beings and, therefore, need others around us to share our lives with.

For those unhappy or sad, holding onto negative emotions and not sharing their feelings is always wrong. This is a problem for those who are alone or withdrawn from others. We should encourage anyone alone to find an outlet to offload their feelings. The more we hold our emotions, the worse our mental health becomes.

Some people have a sense of entitlement or feeling owed, especially if they have been spoiled or had deprivation or privation as a child. And for those who feel like this, they need to know that no one owes them anything. We owe it to ourselves to create our best life, as it is not for others to unconditionally do this for us.

Top tip; Make yourself valuable to others, and people will want to be around you. Or even better, make yourself invaluable to others, and you will be deemed priceless. To make this happen, work on doing things that enrich others' lives, which will make you happy at the same time. It's a two-way street to make others want to be around you. Being sincere, reliable, and honest always pays dividends.

Calming your Mind and Reflection

Our bodies require movement and exercise to keep us mobile and active. Because our minds are always busy, they need the opposite, stillness, and rest to help us think clearer and feel calmer. When we stil our minds or practice meditation, we became more peaceful and less stressed. We develop clearer thinking, which stimulates our minds. So here is a simple little exercise to help still your mind and allow you to reflect.

Whole not part

John was married to a lovely gal called Vicky, who was expecting their first baby. She was loyal, kind, and scrubbed up like a rebellious Nun. John successfully owned and managed a car dealership, which he inherited from his father. They lived in a beautiful five-bedroomed colonial style home. They were very fortunate to be so abundant and had all the material possessions anyone could want. Johnny was a bit of a Jack the lad, with a lively character, full chat, and plenty of charm. Vicky had previously been warned that John had some strange ways by his ex-wife but chose to ignore what she had heard, believing her to be jealous.

After visiting her parents, Vicky unexpectedly returned home early. As she walked into the hallway, she caught John admiring himself in front of a full-length mirror, dressed in lingerie and wearing high-heeled shoes. Vicky was pretty shocked as one would expect and particularly horrified to see her new stiletto shoes being stretched three sizes. She had a bit of a rant and, out of anger, told him that she would tell his work colleagues and friends what had happened. John became defensive and strongly warned her not to say a word to anybody; clearly, he wasn't willing to share her lingerie with anyone else. Becoming more suspicious, she started to play detective.

The next day, while John was at work, she took his laptop to the local computer store and had some software installed that would allow her to monitor his activity. A few weeks later, she was horrified to find out that his hallway catwalk was not a one-off. He belonged to an online group called "Sassy Husbands," where they would share pictures, experiences and engage in video activity. After this and not knowing what to do, she confronted him and moved into the guest room. Soon after, John started to become controlling and aggressive towards her, and they had many fights. She became fearful of him, regretting not listening or investigating the advice she was given from his ex-wife. Enough was enough, and so she packed her bags and moved into her elderly parent's home. John came home from work that day to find a letter on the countertop with a pair of stockings attached, which read;

Dear John,

I guess you will need these stockings a lot more than me now, so here is my contribution to your next fancy dress fantasy. I have taken my personal belongings, including all of my underwear and lingerie, so at some point, you will need to mince into town and buy your own. And by the way, don't worry, I haven't told anyone else just yet. Sincerely, Victoria's Secret.

This not only made him furious but very concerned about the potential embarrassment he may have to face from his friends and employees should she say anything. To cover himself, he told everyone that he had thrown his wife out for having an affair with the pool guy, which of course, was not true. Vicky had only told her parents and brother about what had happened, but somehow it got back to John, who went ballistic. He turned up at her parents' home, furious and intoxicated. He was spotted sneakily peering through the back window like a boss-eyed spy. Seeing him, Vicky refused to let him in. Still, he barged in and grabbed her by the neck, warning her to retract her story and admit the affair to everyone or else.

A few days later, she met up with a coffee friend called Vera, who asked her why she had left her husband. I thought you had everything, a cool husband, a beautiful home and car, and a holiday home in Europe. I mean, are you crazy? Vicky sat silent for a moment and then replied, "I thought I did too, you could only see a part of my life, just as I could only see a part of his, and trust me; I have seen the full picture now. I am pregnant, heartbroken, humiliated, and now I am under threat. How can my life change like this in one week? I figured out my mistake Vera was that I should have had my eyes wider open and looked at the situation as a whole, and not as a part when I first met him."

Looking at things in part and not as a whole can often be a mistake that few are aware of and can easily lead us into a false sense of security. When we put ourselves into situations without looking at the bigger picture, we increase the potential of a problematic or even a catastrophic problem that we could have avoided further down the road. It is a common practice for most of us to judge others by image. For the most part, this is fine unless you plan to engage in some commitment with that person. Those who want to impress others will often be well-practiced to make a great first impression and appear credible. When we decide to commit to something, we cannot know the full implications of a decision. Hence, it's about when making your best decision to look beyond the surface and gain more information and facts about that person or situation. Our choices can be crucial, so the more effort we put into making sure that we get it right, the better.

Learning about those that are Streetwise

Those who are raised in homes or environments where there is a need to be sharp to survive will likely develop the art of being streetwise. Like everything, some are better than others as abilities and skillsets vary from person to person. When parents or caregivers allow children the freedom to go off and do whatever they want outside of the home, they are likely to experience problematic or even dangerous situations. And those experiences teach them to be streetwise, especially if they live or hang out with the wrong crowd in the wrong area; For some, it can be a jungle out there.

It is sad but true that there are people who will always try to take advantage of others in some way, especially those who are living in challenging circumstances.

Being streetwise can be a fabulous tool to have, particularly in city life or under challenging environments and a skill that every child would benefit from learning. Being streetwise is developing the ability to protect yourself from being taken advantage of and manipulating odds in your favor to gain the best outcome in any given situation. To be streetwise, you have to know how to play the game. Have a sharp nose for a deal, recognize danger and opportunity, and react in a heartbeat. You will have to think quickly on your feet, knowing when to get in and when to stay put. How to bend the rules, and break them if required? And sense or recognize a shady character or situation when it is in front of you.

Unfortunately, some of those who are streetwise can be "fly or cute." This means they can be manipulative, dishonest, and deceitful and intend to get what they want regardless of the other person's needs or feelings. These are people to avoid at all costs because they can easily pull the wool over your eyes for gain and often lack conscience.

There are many situations in life when someone who is streetwise has an advantage over someone who is not and, of course, vice versa. Those that have had the good fortune of a nurtured upbringing will often be more secure, better educated, and more grounded. And this is excellent fortune, except those who are not streetwise are much more likely to be manipulated by others, fall for scams, and generally struggle in strenuous or challenging situations. Those that have learned the skills of reading people and problem solving will duck and dive as necessary. They manage stress and challenge better and are often highly skilled in the art of negotiation and wise avoidance. They know when and how to bluff and seem to get through situations bruised but not battered because of learned resilience. Those that are streetwise use a lot of body language, slang, and banter, all of which have essential benefits in this dog eat dog world that many live in.

Top tip; Streetwise, people make great friends - assuming they are honest. They will bring sound advice and brilliant problem-solving solutions when needed. They are generally exciting people to hang out with. Streetwise, individuals tend to have a lot of character.

Top tip; Those who achieve a respected status in a particular subject or field do so because they practice their natural abilities with effort and determination. Be nothing more than pure determination, and know that you can make anything happen if you want it enough and are prepared to go get it. If you do not achieve something, it will be because you didn't work hard enough, which really means that you didn't want it enough.

The Power of Forgiveness

Jane had recently lost her dog, Gordon, a 15-year-old Beagle that she had adopted 10 years previously from the local rescue center. His first owner Stuart trained Gordon to smell money. His theory was a belief that criminals hid illegal cash in woodlands, away from their homes, and that he could find it. He would go out dog walking each day, searching for hidden money. His months of training proved lucrative, until when on one particular occasion, they were caught digging up money that belonged to a gang of ruthless drug dealers. He recognized them from seeing them around town, and so grabbing his pitchfork, he and Gordon ran off as fast as possible, pursued by three men. Fearing for his life, he managed to get some headway and dived into an alleyway. Gordon started to bark, and Stuart, who was panting like a desperate housewife in the front row of a Chippendales show, went into a full-blown panic attack. Letting go of Gordon's leash while falling to his knees, a cat ran by, and Gordon went after it. Stuart chased after him in his panic, breathlessly screaming Gor, Gor. Still, it sounded like Whore. Stuart was running up the street with a pitchfork in his left-hand yelling Whore, Whore, which of course, attracted plenty of unwanted attention. Eventually, the cat got away, and Gordon stopped running. A police officer noted what was going on and approached him. Stuart explained that his dog had chased a cat, and with that, Gordon jumped up at the police officer sniffing his pockets. Stuart pulled Gordon off, apologized, and sheepishly walked off, petting Gordon through gritted teeth.

A couple of days later, Stuart's door knocked, and looking through the window, he saw that it was one of the men that were chasing him, so he had to leave town quickly. And that's how Gordon ended up in the rescue center and with Alice.

He was a sweet dog, but he had an attitude, and taking him for a walk proved challenging. He would start howling whenever he passed a bank and would jump up at passersby sniffing money in their pockets. The worst moment was when Alice almost got arrested after Gordon attacked the man transporting cash from the supermarket to his vehicle. Trying to help, she was accused of attempting to commit a hold-up robbery.

Alice was terrified of ATM's as Gordon was obsessed by them and would spend her time always looking for ATM's to avoid and would have to cross the street if she saw one coming up.

Because of this, Alice rarely ventured outside with Gordon due to his overwhelming desire to find cash. Still, she completely stopped after the local mechanic had four sutures in his head when Gordon attacked his groin while he was working under a car. After that, she was extra careful explaining to everyone entering her house not to bring in any money.

Gordon was Alice's best friend, but he sadly passed away due to natural causes. Alice was absolutely devastated and began to withdraw and hide away from others. Her daughter Claire became worried about her after receiving a call from her Mother's neighbor expressing concern. She sent her husband, David, to check on her and make sure that she was OK. They held a key, and after knocking on the door without a reply, he accessed the property.

Alice was in the lounge alone and sat idle. The house was in disarray with dirty dishes piled up on the side and mess everywhere. It was unusual as Alice had always been a tidy house-proud person. David kindly asked her if she was OK and if she needed help with anything, explaining that he and Claire were worried about her. Being furious with David for entering her property, she yelled at him. "How dare you come into my home uninvited" and continued to barrage him with insults telling him "what a trash son-in-law he was." And how, "after 18 years, she was still puzzled as to why her daughter married such a wimpy stupid little man."

David was sensitive, and this incident really upset him. Keeping his mouth shut, he left quietly and returned home. Telling Claire what had happened he went into a rant, stating how much he has done for her Mother over the years. "How dare she insult me like that" he yelled as he walked out into the garden to cool down. David took it badly and became very bitter towards Alice and could not let it drop. Claire kept telling him to let it go, reminding him that her Mother was not in a good place mentally after losing her beloved dog. Time went on, and David could not find it in himself to forgive her, and the resentment continued to build. Alice even apologized to David, but it wasn't good enough. It became a constant source of a quarrel between him and Claire, causing friction and complications. He even refused to go to any family events where Alice would be. Things got so bad that and he ended up receiving counseling.

David explained everything to the counselor, who suggested that forgiving his Mother in law was about him, not her. That it was his life that was falling apart due to the upset and anguish, he was carrying. He told him that by forgiving, he would become the beneficiary, not the victim. "Look," he said, "Say you have had an argument or a bad experience with a friend or family member, which had left you feeling aggrieved. You leave the situation upset and are unable to stop thinking about it. Then you continue to dwell on it for days, weeks, months, and in some cases for years. You no longer speak with that person, and your anger verges on hatred. The mere mention of that person's name or any reminder can cause you to scowl like a rabid dog. It brings a flood of emotion back to the surface, and each time you have these triggers, the hurt returns. Suppose that person apologized to you, stating how sorry they were and asked for forgiveness. By forgiving them, you will have removed all of that anguish. Those who do not forgive continue to carry pain and suffering, and all because of someone else's actions. Again, ask yourself, what part did you play in it?

When we apportion part of the blame on ourselves, we are less likely to feel so aggrieved. Unless, of course, you are taking all of the responsibility, in which case, ask yourself what part the other person played it in so that you can apportion some of the blame on them. Remember that there are three sides to every story, his, hers, and the truth.

The counselor then shared some stories about his old dog and how that dog changed his life from living dishonest and dangerous to becoming a counselor and helping others. He also shared how angry and upset he had become when he lost his dog due to a mistake some 10 years earlier. Still, that mistake changed his life for the better, and in training to become a counselor, he learned to forgive others as well as himself.

David finally recognized the importance of forgiveness, not just to his Mother in law but toward anyone who had previously hurt or upset him.

The counselor's name happened to be Stuart, and his dog that he lost 10 years prior was a beagle called Gordon.

There is always positive learning in every adverse event. Something positive will have happened due to the experience, regardless of how bad it was, as all negative experiences bring positive knowledge, albeit not pleasant. Don't become stuck in the thinking, why should I forgive, because that person doesn't deserve my forgiveness? This is a mistake that many people make; let it go; all that matters is your personal, immediate, and future happiness. It doesn't mean that you need to make up, befriend, or have them back in your life, perhaps they do not deserve that, and it doesn't mean that you need to forget. It means that you will gain closure in the forgiving, and in that closure, you are allowing yourself to move on. Forgiveness is about allowing yourself to be at peace because life is too short to hold grudges.

For those people carrying anger, bitterness, or resentment, there is a way to shift those feelings.

Practice; This subconscious cleansing of forgiveness and learning promotes closure. It would be best if you did this individually for each issue.

Find a quiet space and sit comfortably. Using a piece of paper and a pen, draw a horizontal line across the page. Starting with the number one up to the age you are now, write them across the line (allowing gaps). Each number represents an age. Spend some time remembering events that had left you upset and hurt in the past and write down the person's name or initials above the age you were when it happened. With your arms crossed, rub the back of your arms from your shoulder down to your elbow, and back up to your shoulder in an up & down rhythm. Keep doing this for the duration of the exercise. Now imagine yourself floating over the line and seeing yourself remembering the event. Once you have done this, take a moment to find the positive learning from the event. (There will be one) And once you have done this, say out loud what that positive lesson was, and I forgive you (Name) for the hurt, pain, and distress you caused me. I thank you for the experience and the learning, and I release you with love.

It is as easy as that and will make you feel much better, then, if necessary, move onto the next person who has caused you upset.

Misery loves Company

Alan was on his way to an interview for a head gardener position at the local garden center. It was a job he had really wanted and had told all of his friends that he genuinely felt he could see himself working there. On the application form, he stated that he was a natural gardener. Although what he didn't say was that his gardening experience was based on successfully growing weed in his trailer, which he had been doing for years. He was a carefree fella about town, well-known and loveable. That said, he was a little naive: he thought aromatic ducks came from Dubai, and algebra was a holiday destination near Dubai.

Running late, he wasn't having the best of starts to the day after ruining his only pair of sneakers by cleaning them with a metal scouring pad. Rarely washing his truck and, for entertainment purposes, he had drawn a hilarious face in the side windows, leaving gaps for his eyes. Whenever he looked out of the window, others would see just his eyes peering through a goofy face. He had also written in the dirt on the back of the car; I bet you wish your truck was as filthy as my wife, but what he meant to write was; I bet you wish that your wife was as dirty as my truck.

Seeing an old friend that he hadn't seen for ages while stopping at a gas station, he shouted over, "congratulations on your pregnancy Margie." Still, she wasn't pregnant, so she yelled back, "go do one." Then, in his rush, he inadvertently stepped ahead of another guy to quickly pay for his fuel and ran out the door shouting "sorry." A few moments later, he noticed that the same guy was following him in a vehicle behind. When Alan reduced his speed looking for the turn, the other driver started to blast his horn, shouting and shaking his fist. Alan was a short man who wore thick-rimmed glasses and carried a very non-threatening appearance. The guy threatening was huge, burly, and aggressive. He pulled alongside, and Alan peered through the gaps of the window drawing to see him, which on this occasion did not make the other person laugh or smile. Alan then proceeded to unwind his window and duly gave him a "birdy" before speeding off.

He arrived at his destination, and the big guy caught up with him again. Immediately he jumped out of his vehicle and stomped over. He demanded Alan got out of his car and started kicking the door and spitting at the window. Not wanting his window artwork damaged, Alan swiftly slid over and got out through the passenger door. An altercation followed, and Alan decked the burly guy in about 10 seconds flat, and while stood over him, he shouted, "go pick on someone your own size, big boy." The bully didn't know that little Alan had been doing competition kickboxing and martial arts for over 20 years; suffice to say that he was pretty handy. Unfortunately for Alan, it had attracted attention from the garden center offices, including the person who would have interviewed him for the job. Within moments the police arrived, and they were both arrested. Still, Alan proclaimed his innocence, which didn't hold water with the officer, given that the other guy was laid out on the floor like a hopeless drunk wearing a glass of cranberry juice. No matter how hard he tried, he was unable to convince the officer differently.

Both were placed in handcuffs and taken off to jail. He was placed on bail, and three months later, he was hauled in front of the judge, where he was sentenced to a thousand dollar fine and 100 hours community service.

His placement for community service; At the local garden center. His task; Assisting the newly appointed head gardener/grower.

After the event, Alan realized that he had another person spread their misery onto him in allowing someone else to control his emotions. It had cost him a potential job, a criminal conviction, a night in jail. Plus three months on bail, a fine of a thousand dollars, and 100 hours of unpaid work with the person who got the job that should have been his. All of which could have been easily avoided with a bit of self-control. After this lesson, Alan always avoids these situations and no longer allows himself to become involved or angry in response to what someone else says or is doing.

Food for Thought

Unless it's criminal, unethical, or dangerous, do we have the right to be angry with someone else just because we do not like or agree with what they are doing? Of course, the answer is no; we have no right to tell others what to do. When someone becomes annoyed or angry with another person for no valid reason, they struggle to manage their feelings. Road rage is just one example of this, but there are many. Causing harm to others for no reason other than the fact that you are angry is unacceptable and profoundly disrespectful. It can be extremely distressing and damaging to the recipient. This is a form of emotional abuse and causes damage. We all know how horrible it feels when people hurt us. Not lowering ourselves to their level protects us from further hurt, more frustration and stops us from putting ourselves into compromising or dangerous situations. Suppose we remonstrate a no-harm to others' policy, except in self-defense. In that case, our lives will be calmer and safer, and we can enjoy our freedom with a clear conscience.

A person who feels the need to be mean or aggressive to another suffers inner anger and frustration themselves. It is impossible to be happy if you are angry or upset. So, by not being drawn into retaliation and taking the higher road, you are already the winner by default. Retaliating feeds the aggressor, and so why give them what they want? When used appropriately; Silence is a powerful tool.

When seeking revenge or projecting anger towards another, dig two graves, one for you.

Practice; Havening is a great way to release anger or frustration without hurting those around you. Cross your arms and rub the back of your arms from your shoulders down to your elbows in an up and down stroking manner. As you do this, speak out all your pent up thoughts and frustrations. Keep doing this until the disappointment or anger subsides.

Empathy & Compassion

Empathy is understanding and sharing others' feelings, and compassion is the ability to feel for another. Being kind to others doesn't just make others happier it makes us happier too. It activates an area of the brain called the striatum, which means that those with empathy enjoy a better living experience. Those that lack understanding of others are very unlikely to acquire inner peace or true happiness. And this is one of the reasons why there are so many unhappy wealthy people in the world. People today in western society are too focused on appearing successful and wanting to be admired for what they have materialistically. Those who are genuinely kind and compassionate help others for the sake of helping others, not to feed their egos, ease their conscience, or look good. And people do notice this, even if they do not say so.

Today, many people have role models that have fame, power, wealth, and beautiful appearances. And we idolize them regardless of how empathetic, kind, caring, or fair they may be. Lack of empathy breeds selfishness, and selfishness brings isolation and loneliness in the end. You can be lonely in a room full of people because loneliness is a state of mind. It is a condition often caused by the way we interact or treat others. Those with compassion and empathy will always be more content, have and hold meaningful relationships, and live steadier lives. Those that do not care about others and only themselves can never have real success. Let me ask you a question. Is a person making millions of dollars and paying his staff the minimum wage kind, empathetic, or compassionate? When admiring these traits in people who lack compassion and empathy, we encourage egocentric and selfish behavior, causing an epidemic of mental health issues.

Rapport with Others

Talk is the ticket that takes you everywhere in life. Using the right words at the right time is real power. It connects you to others, navigates your chosen path, and makes dreams come true. Some people have a natural ability to do this successfully. Still, those who don't can learn rapport-building communication skills.

Practice; If we want to make a good impression when we meet up with someone we do not know or do not know well, we should speak in a similar or parrot-fashion manner to build rapport. Being congruent and using adaptable speech. Phrase sentences in a similar fashion to the other person by picking up keywords they use and copying them. Notice the other person's pace of speech; is it quick, moderate, or slow? Unless you mimic the other person, don't go all around the houses to say what you want to say, be concise and to the point. If you're going to tell someone you have popped to the shop and bought milk, say it just like that and not like this; I walked down the hill and crossed the road. It wasn't busy, so I cut through the park and went to the shop, but there was a line, and then I bought some milk. It sounds boring. Find things in common to talk about by finding a conversation highway; in other words, use wording that prompts a reply. Learn about generic subjects that both males and females can use effectively. Above all, make them feel valued by using sincere compliments, and if you can, use appropriate humor. Smile, and avoid conversations about politics or religion as this can result in friction or disagreement.

Listen carefully to what the other person has to say. After he or she has finished, reaffirm, or clarify something he or she has said. You can do this by nodding your head or by repeating a part of it for further clarification. It shows that you are paying attention and are interested in what they have to say. Do not make the classic mistake of making the conversation all about you. Show interest in them by saying less about yourself unless you are asked or have something that would be helpful, comforting, or in common with them. Your voice should come over warm, friendly, and bright with a variation of pitch. Most women have a natural, pleasing tone to their voice. In contrast, many men have monotone voices, so you may need to develop your pitch variation to sound more engaging. If you are male and suffer from a monotone voice, you can improve this by practicing pitch variation.

Pitch practice; With your voice as low as it can go, start counting. With each number you call out, increase the pitch slightly, getting higher and higher until your voice breaks up or sounds squeaky. Repeat this a couple of times daily for a few weeks.

It's not what you say it's how you say it.

We can subconsciously deliver a message that we are confident using our body language. A strong stance with good posture, feet apart, and using hand gestures will show quiet confidence. When speaking descriptively or explaining something using hand gestures, you will appear more exciting and appealing.

Adopt a relaxed-looking demeanor in your approach. Keep about a meter away to not invade the other person's space and use good body posture. Be mindful of not coming across too strong or cocky. It would be best if you come across as confident but humble and sincere. Always be polite and careful not to be too blunt, sound aggressive, or be overly critical or contrary.

Sometimes we disagree or have a different point of view to others, and that is perfectly acceptable. Still, the delivery is essential to get right, so deliver your words deliberately using facts and emotions when you need it.

If someone said to you, I went to the new restaurant in town last night and had a fabulous meal, and you disagreed; you could reply, "I went there last week too, and I found the service really poor. Do you know that we waited over 15 minutes just to order a drink?" Rather than saying, "The service was rubbish, and I thought the restaurant was awful." If you are saying something that may sound harsh, soften how you say it.

Example: "Guess we picked the wrong night; our experience wasn't as good as yours." Always make a greeting and a goodbye pleasurable for the other person, "Hi, pleased to meet you" or "Hopefully, I will see you again." When saying Hello, Hi, or Goodbye, sound spritely and upbeat and use the person's name if you know it.

While in conversation, be positive and give compliments. When we give compliments, we give praise, which boosts both the person we are praising and yourself. It tells the other person that you like them or like something about them, and that generally makes them like you too. However, it needs to be genuine and not false, as people will see through you. Find something you like about the person or what they are saying so you can pay a sincere compliment.

Perhaps you will want to connect with that person again, and if so, let it be known by saying something like, "hope to see you again soon." Ask for their number if you need it.

Always come across as positive, and when empathizing, tilt your head slightly sideways to accent the emotion.

When shaking hands, always give eye contact and make the handshake firm but not too firm or limp. A medium handshake is still the best as it comes over as the most genuine.

Top tip; Here's a mantra to use before you speak which will help you achieve better rapport. It's called **T.H.I.N.K.** **T** - is it True? **H** - is it Helpful? **I** - is it inspiring? **N** – is it necessary? **K –** is it Kind?

My Way or the Highway

I have observed that many people make their lives complicated because they are not easy-going, causing constant difficulty and inner unrest. They will likely struggle in relationships and in many other areas of their lives. Even when successful, they remain irritable and unhappy. This "my way or the high way attitude" is not conducive to a comfortable, fulfilled life. Society places so much emphasis on success, but it forgets to encourage us to do it with kindness and style. So we have ended up with many narcissists and bullies who have this type of awkward personality.

Top tip; If you feel intimidated and want to appear confident and strong, use this body language.; Stand feet apart and keep good posture with your shoulders back and head upright. Look confidently into the other person's eyes when you are speaking. Looking frightened empowers an aggressor, and so when you look solid and fearless, it causes the other person to be a little more cautious. When speaking, be animated and expressive with your hands. Try to mimic the other person's speech style. Be courteous and friendly; add a smile or a grin.

Suppose you want to protect yourself from a grim situation; you can appear really intimidating by staring directly below their eyes, so you are glaring at their cheekbones. In that case, you will come across as looking a little deranged. It's an excellent way to let someone feel that they need to be wary of you too.

Co-dependency with Others

When we are on an airplane, we are told to place the oxygen mask on our face first before helping others in the event of an emergency. When we overly care about someone, and we, ourselves, feel insecure, we can become co-dependent. Being co-dependent is when our emotions become entangled with someone else's, which is mentally unhealthy. It means that our feelings are at the mercy of another person, which means that we are not in control. In essence, we are living on an emotional rollercoaster. Those that are co-dependent have trouble making decisions in relationships. They need the approval of others before acting in many situations. An example of co-dependency is; when the person you are co-dependent with is sad, so you feel sad also. When they feel happy, you feel happy. When another person's emotions define your mood, you are co-dependent.

When we love someone, we need to be side-by-side, not joined; it doesn't mean that you love any less; it means that your love is healthy. You will not be able to do your best for the other person or yourself if your emotions are tangled up. Together but separate is how all healthy relationships should be. If they are upset, you feel for them and help them not be upset. If they are sad, you remain happy and try to cheer them up, and if they are upset or angry with someone or something, you comfort and support them, not become bitter or angry.

It's always a mistake to give your power to someone else.

Gratitude & Greed

Being grateful promotes feelings of well-being. It is easy to become complacent if used to others giving to us, especially when we already have everything we want or need. Taking things for granted is a lack of appreciation. Those who act in this way may notice that others dislike them, thinking of them as spoilt, selfish, or greedy. Practicing gratitude for the good things we have, no matter how small or big, promotes psychological well-being. Generosity is an act of kindness, whether it's a smile, a compliment, a gift, or something more substantial. Whenever we receive from others, we should feel and express gratitude.

Those of us who live in the Western world are very fortunate to live in such safe times, have warmth, food, water, shelter, and the pleasures that come with it. We live better today than the Kings of the past did, with our luxury cars, centrally heated homes, designer clothing, and technical advancements. We are so very fortunate to be living in an age where we have had peace in our country. As long as we have good health, we have everything. Therefore, we should appreciate and express gratitude for these glorious riches every day. When we do, we further enhance our well-being. Many people look for reasons to complain instead of appreciating the good things we have. As humans, we have an instinct to want more, right from birth, and without the ability to even speak or think, we ask for food by crying when we need it. As we grow older, we further learn to ask for the things we need. Still, then we start to want material things that we do not need because others have them or purely for the sake of wanting.

Greed goes hand in hand with selfishness, and people do not like greedy, selfish people. So being greedy and selfish does come with a price. It causes struggle in relationships, working environments, friendships, and family life because they are not team players. Those living happy, balanced lives recognize and value the importance of being a team player within a unit.

Chapter 7

Awareness of those Around You

Underlying or Presenting

Stanley went to the doctors complaining of a strep throat. The doctor sat him down and examined his throat. He found that it wasn't his throat that was the problem; it was an abscess right at his mouth's back.

"You have an abscess; perhaps you are run down, Stanley"? Said the doctor.

"Well, I have been feeling under the weather lately, but I have not been sleeping well either, to be honest."

"Right, well, lack of sleep is not good for any of us, is it?"

"Probably not; I've been going through a tough time of late. My marriage is on the rocks, and I have had a lot on my mind."

"I am sorry to hear that, Stanley, but I am sure it will all work out for you."

"Thanks, but my marriage hasn't been working for years."

"Why don't you get a divorce if it's troubling you that much?"

"The thing is that I am terrified of being on my own."

Stanley went to the doctor with a presenting problem of what he thought was a strep throat. After investigation, the doctor found that the underlying issue wasn't the throat, abscess, lack of sleep, or marriage problems. Stanley's real issue was that he was terrified of being alone.

Whenever we experience a presenting problem, there is often an underlying issue. When we deal with the presenting problem we are not solving the real issue. To solve matters permanently, we must figure out what the root cause of a situation is. And this will be the underlying cause.

The Three Personalities

There are lots of personality tests available that go into great detail about an individual's traits. To help understand someone, we can place a person into three personality types using a psychoanalytic Freudian method. The three personality traits are; Anal, Oral, and Hysteria.

We can all have a mix of these personality traits. Still, we will all have one dominant characteristic, which places us into one of these three personality types. Once you have worked out what a person's personality type is, it will afford you a shortcut to understanding that person and how that person works without knowing much about them.

Type Oral are genuine, thoughtful, and sensitive individuals who keep a low profile and care about others. This type of personality is more likely to suffer from anxiety-related disorders. They hold emotions internally and do not share their feelings readily. This builds up and makes them more anxious, causing them to overthink, worry, and suffer low moods.

Type Anal is a more robust individual who is less sensitive and more pragmatic. Often lacking sensitivity when they become frustrated or angry, they release by yelling and blaming others but can quickly recover and move on. They can be short-tempered, aggressive, and lack understanding. But with that said, they are less likely to hold a grudge once they have calmed down.

Type Hysteria is dramatic and theatrical and the natural actors of life, and therefore, always wanting attention in some way. They have sensitivity, but their situations will always be worse and more important than anyone else's. They can adapt, change, cry at the drop of a hat, and are often unpredictable. They do, however, recover from situations quickly but are generally shallow.

Personality Mix

Anal with Anal types are likely to have fierce or fiery relationships but recover quickly. Anal types struggle to understand the sensitivity of others and therefore put their feelings first.

Anal with Oral types together is common. The Oral type feels secure to have someone more outgoing and single-minded. The Anal type finds the Oral type easier and less demanding. However, Oral types can become deeply hurt when an Anal style says something hurtful and struggles to understand why the Oral personality style takes so long to recover. They become emotionally injured due to their sensitive persona and heal slower, unlike the Anal type.

Oral and Oral types together will have a calm and peaceful relationship, both respecting the other person's needs and sensitivities. However, suppose both Oral types suffer from an anxiety disorder. In that case, it is likely to worsen as they can easily feed each other's fear and negativity.

Anal and Hysteria types together would be entertaining initially. Still, the Anal style may end up finding the drama of the hysteria person very frustrating. The Hysteria type would benefit from the discipline of an Anal kind who could keep him or her in check.

Hysteria with Hysteria types is likely to be entertaining but competitive, dramatic, and intense. Both parties demand attention and are prone to being unstable and unpredictable.

Oral and Hysteria types are sensitive, so they have plenty of things in common things and are often compatible. However, the Oral may prefer them in small doses as they may tire of drama. The Hysteria might find it to be a monotonous or dull relationship.

Judging on Appearances

Those studying Ph.D.'s or Doctorates are trained to learn to use factual information only. A doctor does not guess a diagnosis but searches for evidence and proof to confirm the medical problem. If he or she is not sure, then it will be passed to someone who can investigate further, perhaps for an x-ray or a consultant who is an expert in that field. Know that many a ripened apple has a rotten core, and we need to consider more than image when we judge someone. There are many examples of false appearances. Unfortunately, the world is plentiful of fake people that use appearance or image to manipulate others for self-satisfaction. We should stay open-minded in our judgments until trust is learned or earned. We can see people who are blessed with external beauty to find out that they are ugly on the inside, or visually unattractive people to find beautiful on the inside.

Many comedians suffer depression, comedy is a serious business, and many people act tough when weak. And I am sure you too can think of many other examples like this. Still, the bottom line is judging anyone or anything by appearance alone is a mistake and can lead us into a false economy. Before we decide, we should always look below the surface because all that glitters is not gold.

Chapter 8

Setting out your Manifesto

Champion Mind-Set

Success for those who manifest, nurture and practice their gift, and everyone has a gift. Heading forward without direction will surely get you lost. When we decide to do a makeover in our home, we start by clearing the rooms, perhaps we strip back the old wallpaper, and then we sand down the paintwork. Then we fill all the holes and gaps before applying the new paint. Perhaps we add some new carpets and furnishings too.

This metaphor is also right for those who want real positive change in their life because it requires preparation and effort to remodel thinking. Those with champion mindsets do not allow fear-based thinking to stop them from achieving. They do not doubt their ability or dwell on thoughts such as; What if I quit my job and can't get another? What if I can't pay the rent or mortgage? What if I leave and I am lonely? What will people think of me? This fear-based negative thinking limits us and stops us from living the life we want. Things always work out best for those that make the best of the way things work out. We all have the same amount of hours in a day, as does every person on the planet. You have the opportunity to do whatever you choose to do with your time. When aspiring to be like others, make sure they are good role models. Unfortunately, many admire tough, and rigid people, which then encourages us to behave in a similar manner. Those that act in this way may end up consumed with bitterness. The only route to inner happiness is to be full of love. The more we love, the happier we feel. Those who use fear or intimidation must be unkind, selfish, and egotistic.

By now, you should have learned a great deal about yourself and others. Your working process of change and the learning should be moving along nicely, building yourself a happy and more fulfilled state of mind. In life, your attitude will dictate your altitude, and a positive and determined approach will take you anywhere you choose to go.

Often you will hear people say to find a mentor and follow him or her, and I agree that this is a great thing. I am indeed mentoring you now, but you don't have to have just one person as a mentor; you can have several. You can copy certain traits and characteristics and learn from those you admire, taking a little something from each person. This way, you don't have to feel like your cloning or trying to be someone else, so you can create a unique new you. Achievement and success mean something different to each person. You do not have to be tough on others to become successful, nor do you have to be cheap to achieve financial abundance.

Those with uncompromising and bullish attitudes may make money. Still, they will not be well-liked, and it is hard to see how anyone can be truly successful if they are not well-liked. Being well-liked is rarely thought of as a success. Yet, it is one of the most beneficial achievements one can have because of what the power admiration brings. It gives us sincere friends, genuine respect, opportunities, good times, joy, pleasure, and happiness. Suppose you have plenty of people wishing you well and thinking positively towards you. Now take a moment to think about the good fortune of all that positive energy being directed at you.

Practice; Boost your determination with this motivational visualization.

Imagine a huge Ox with big horns sat in front of you. It's one massive beast. Take a few moments to think about the specific issue that you require motivation for, and think about your lack of achievement or discipline in the past. Add in any disappointment, hurt or pain that you have endured as a result of the failure, and intensify those feelings. Now visualize that issue being absorbed into the body of that Ox. Then using your imagination, visualize yourself taking a hold of the Ox by the horns. With aggression and determination, say out loud: I will show you (name) or the world how strong and disciplined I am and what I can do. I can and will achieve this because it means that much to me. It means more than anything to me that I can do this. My reputation is in question here. Spin the Ox around and around by the horns like an athlete would when throwing a discus in an Olympic event. Toss it far into the distance and visualize it flying miles and miles until you can no longer see it anymore. As you do this intensify positive feelings and command yourself: That's how strong I have become, I can and will achieve this, now watch me fly Universe. Nothing is going to stop me. It means the absolute world to me to achieve this and it's a measure of my calibre as a person. Visualize yourself having achieved it and immediately set to work on what ever it is that you wanted the motivation for. For a full guided visualization listen to **Hypnosis audio download 003 Motivational Booster**

Reputation

Whenever we have a disagreement or sever a relationship with someone, it is always a mistake to completely burn your bridges. To say things over and beyond what is necessary will cause long-term damage to relationships and your reputation. When we go overboard on others, they will lose respect for you. They may forgive, but rarely will they forget. Even if you feel the cause of the situation is someone else's fault, never cause irrevocable and permanent damage. You never know who someone is connected to or what might happen in the future.

It is vitally important to be aware of how others perceive you and are critical to your reputation. Your reputation opens and closes doors of opportunity, and those with dignity prosper more than those without. A good reputation takes time and effort to acquire. It can be lost in a moment of madness and should be guarded at all costs because what others think about you can matter if it's harmful.

Top Tip; If you have a tarnished reputation, get to work on changing it. Once you start to act differently, people will see you differently, and your status will improve. Guard this fiercely as this is a crucial aspect of life that many people overlook. Being respected by others is essential if you want to be around good people, so refrain from situations that can harm your reputation. Be careful how you treat others, including children, as they are the adults of tomorrow. Their opinion of you will form during childhood and may matter significantly in the future. Stay loyal and consistent and be a person of your word.

Work Ethic

A professional athlete who dreams of winning, knows how much effort it requires for even a chance of doing well in a competition. Sometimes we can work really hard at something and end up with nothing or even make a loss. This is very disappointing and more so if you realize that you have been a busy fool. It's all about learning from mistakes and working towards your goal diligently and consistently. Working smart is not taking short cuts; it is streamlining hard work. It's having the right people, help, or advice around you when you need it, especially for the parts you do not understand or struggle to manage. A continuous improvement program is essential for learning, developing, keeping up to date investing in things that can aid or enhance what you do and how you do it. And so it comes down to investment; the more you put in, the more you get out. Even if sometimes its only experience, it will increase the chances of success next time. No one achieves anything without working at it. The more successful you want to be, the more challenging it will be. If you want real success in any area of your life, you will have to give your all.

Destination

If we look at any goal as a destination instead of a sub destination, we are more likely to give up or undo the hard work we have put in once we have achieved it. An athlete trains hard, but for that athlete to keep winning, after celebrating, he must get straight back onto his journey, looking for his next sub-destination. A salesperson will look for the next deal, a writer the next book, a builder the next build. This applies to all people's goals and ambitions. Although attaining any goal is very commendable, it invariably leads to another. Therefore we should be viewing our goals as sub-destinations and not final destinations.

Celebrating the achievements of each sub destinations is essential, meaningful, and rewarding. Still, a winner's mindset is to celebrate and then shift their attention to the next goal: to maintain, repeat, improve, or attain something new. Life is a journey, so the only real destination we have is the one we reach at the end of our lives.

Top tip; Seeing destinations as sub-destinations dramatically increases the likelihood of being successful. Be aware also that success and overall happiness are two different things. A person who is focused only on making money may very well gain financial abundance. Still, without investing in other aspects of their lives, they are likely to experience some misery to accompany their wealth. Investing in several parts of one's life, such as relationships, friends, family, and mental and physical health, is essential for happiness.

Be sure to reward yourself positively whenever you complete a goal. A reward can be anything from a pat on the back to a treat or gift. Upon completion of a goal, immediately move to your next sub-destination, letting go of the previous achievement so that your focus on the following is equal or more robust than the last.

Achieving Goals

The people you mix with have a considerable influence on your quality of life and reflect who you are. Choose wisely those you decide to spend your precious time with, making sure they bring something positive to the table. If they don't make you happy or bring misery or negativity into your life, do something about it. If you are not progressing or are continuing to do what you have always done, you will get the same results. You cannot expect to see a change if you do not make one. Those that chase much catch few. Be focused on achieving one thing at a time, rather than using a scattergun approach and spreading yourself too thin. When you work on one main goal, you will reach your destination quicker and do a better job because you will be more concentrated. We are naturally drawn to the things that we enjoy, and we want the things that we are naturally drawn to. We humans are not interested in pursuing things that do not come naturally to us or are not good at. If you are interested in something, you will be able to do it well with practice.

Consistency

Those that achieve success do so because they stay consistent in their endeavors. They keep at things in a focused, steady, and productive manner, which brings them achievement and reward. Those who waver, keep changing their minds, or start other projects before finishing another will likely struggle to find the success they desire. When analyzing anyone who has made it to the top or been successful, you can be sure that they have worked hard and stayed consistent. They have also reviewed their decisions along the way because tweak and change is an important part of progress. Achieving goals brings inner happiness, promoting feelings of joy, confidence, credibility, and admiration from others. Those who are not consistent are less likely to feel satisfied and be thought of by others as flaky or unreliable.

Guaranteed Success

The perception of success is individual to each person's goals and desires. Some seek victory in one particular field, such as career, financial, family, or academic. For others, it may be a combination of different things. Whatever your desires and goals are, there will be specific requirements necessary to ensure you achieve success. One of the main reasons people fail is that they give up or change direction far too quickly. Those who have a never-give-up attitude, commit to working hard at something they are passionate about and care about continuous improvement cannot fail. To achieve the right level of success in anything, you will need unstoppable motivation for what you do because you will encounter many obstacles, difficulties, and challenges along the way. It's tough to be successful doing something that you do not enjoy, and even though you might make money at it, it is unlikely you will feel happy. Without happiness, it is a debatable claim to say you are truly successful. When doing something you are passionate about, you dramatically increase the odds of success because you enjoy the journey. And this is extremely important if your motivation wains or you have distractions to deal with. All trips for success are long.

No matter how hard something may appear, there is always a solution -you just have to find it.

Making your Investment Count.

Generally, we do not jump from an awful situation to a great one, as it's a gradual process. We progress in stages, improving little by little. The piece representing where you are now must be positioned into place; otherwise, the next section will not fit. Whatever your desire for your future is, you have to ensure that you are getting the piece in the now right to move forward. Otherwise, you will find your plans failing, or it taking a lot longer than you anticipated. We have all lost and missed out on opportunities and relationships due to a lack of investment. If you want to be in charge of your future, you have to invest in yourself and others. Those who do not invest in themselves or others will miss out on many opportunities, have fewer friends and fun times, distant families, and be less liked by others. Investing in others will enhance your life, bringing you more friends, opportunities, personal satisfaction, and good times. Investing in your family, friends, physical and mental health, home, career or job, hobbies, or other essential things for your well-being and happiness requires positive investment.

Know that if you are working and investing your skill and time for someone else, you are building their dream, not yours, which is fine, but it does need to fulfil your plan or dream too, whatever that may be. Anything in the past that has not worked out has not been a mistake, it's been a step towards where you are today, and today is a step towards where you will be tomorrow. Successful people maximize their opportunities, so when you find a favorable option which is going well, invest more because the more you invest, the bigger the dividend. Thinking in the now and deciding what you want for the future allows you to put the building blocks in place and dramatically increases your chances of achieving it.

Relying on hope or wishing for your dreams to come true is not enough to make them realize. A destination requires a planned route - without a map, you have a much less chance of getting there. To say, I'm going to be, or I'm going to have is not enough. It's like saying that you will own a Ferrari and not figuring out how you will afford to buy it, let alone run it.

Whatever your goals, dreams, or aspirations are, lets start by making a list of what they are. Make your plan using these categories: Material, Career, Financial, Personal, Physical, Mental, Emotional, and Spiritual.

Add more detail, i.e., Type of house and the location you would like to live in, the car or cars you would like to drive, how much money you want to earn, what countries you want to visit, etc. You can modify this anytime, as things and situations do change.

Note your behavior, and whether it contributes toward a positive or a negative outcome for the future. Each positive investment will move you towards the goal you have set in that particular category. And each negative investment will push it further away. So whatever it is that you want, positively invest.

To create my personal manifesto plan, I spent some time considering exactly what I wanted. I listed my goals in the following categories;: career, personally, spiritually, mentally, and physically.

I wanted to achieve in my long-term plan, and knowing how things change and evolve, working in 6-month increments. This gave me a lot more control over the outcome and makes progress more manageable and less overwhelming. I looked at every movement I made with an investment mindset, which allowed me to be sure whether I was investing positively or negatively towards my goals.

By attaching an investment value to each thing you do, you will differentiate what will help reach your goals and not. For example, let's say one of your goals was to run a marathon. Suppose you smoked 20 cigarettes a day, didn't exercise, and regularly binged on junk food; clearly this would be a negative investment.

Practice: It's time now to create your plan. Spend some time deciding on the things that you want for your future happiness and a fulfilled life. Go big on these, and make sure that they do not conflict. With a pen and paper, list out your goals, dreams, and desires. I have created an example below to get you started.

You can revisit this periodically to tweak or change as necessary because things do change. Don't stick with a plan if it's not working.

Create your vision board in each these areas, and then add detail.

Career	**Goal**	**How**	**When by**
Personally	**Goal**	**How**	**When by**
Materialistically	**Goal**	**How**	**When by**
Physically	**Goal**	**How**	**When by**
Mentally	**Goal**	**How**	**When by**

Chapter 9

The Universal Boomerang

In Out & Back

If the universe is vibrational energy, then it is a force that can deliver whatever it wants to anyone at any time. Imagine if you could manipulate this to work better for you so that anything you want becomes possible. You could make your wishes and dreams come true. Whatever your beliefs may or may not be, most agree that some kind of power exists far more significant than us. It is an energy force that controls many aspects of life itself. Universal power has laws and rules just like any other type of energy force, and we are all plugged in. It applies to everything we do, which is why we should always give significant attention to the implications of our behaviors.

We all reap the consequences of our actions. If we practice malicious behavior, we receive adverse outcomes, and in the practice of positive doings, we obtain favorable results. Those walking down the street swaggering their shoulders projecting aggression are certain to attract aggression. And those projecting love and kindness will attract love and kindness

The universal boomerang reflects our vibration, which is heard and responded to by universal laws. Every action has a reaction and comes with a price or a prize. We get back what we put out.

It does not discriminate and follows the pattern of a boomerang, out and back to you. Not always instant, but in its own time, not always in order but when it's ready.

Anger and aggression will manifest drama and retribution. Selfishness and greed and will manifest false friends and relationships, jealousy, and in the end, probable loneliness. On the other hand, by practicing love, compassion, kindness, forgiveness, and empathy, we manifest real friendships, meaningful relationships, happiness, harmony, inner peace, and positive reward.

Have you ever wondered why it is that when you are needy or desperate, the likelihood getting what you want decreases significantly? Or when you think that negative situations are going to happen, they do. Whatever our thoughts, feelings, needs, and desires are, we consciously or subconsciously project energy. And this energy that we put out into the universe comes back to us, just like a boomerang. When we are overly concerned about events and outcomes, desperate or needy, the energy we are sending out is negative. And this is why it returns a negative result. When we hope for the best, are confident and relaxed about the outcome, we significantly increase the chances of winning.

With this knowledge, I have learned that I choose to let go anytime I feel aggrieved about a person or situation. I do this and believe that the universe will deliver its own retribution to that person or situation in its own time. In working this way, not only am I refusing to allow another person or situation to affect my happiness, I am avoiding negative vibration by return. Drama is always worth avoiding.

We can make our journey more comfortable and less complicated by; minding our own business, acting appropriately, choosing wisely, accepting conditions, and working hard. And this makes for a more comfortable passage through life. Making life as pleasurable as possible is the aim of the game, and miracles can happen. There are millions of undiscovered things being invented all the time that will improve and extend our life's experience. Anything can happen. Today people recover, overcome, and achieve the most incredible things in the most unimaginable ways. We live in a world where a person with a speech impediment can become a TV broadcaster. A person without the ability to sing can become a rock star. A person impaired or disabled can win an Olympic medal. A construction contractor from New York can become the President of America. The possibilities are endless to those that positively believe in what can be achieved using the power of universal energy.

Manifestation is an inherent ability in all of us, and when used correctly, it is a gift. When we work at something, we are willing it to happen. Success is always positive. To manifest, we must ask, be definite in our intention, be positive, believe, and feel that it will happen. It' is a practice. When we have provided enough, we receive what we have asked for or an even better alternative.

Gratitude & Greed

Being grateful promotes feelings of well-being.

It is easy to become complacent if used to others giving to us, especially when we already have everything we want or need. Taking things for granted is a lack of appreciation. Those who act in this way may notice that others dislike them, thinking of them as spoilt, selfish, or greedy. Practicing gratitude for the good things we have, no matter how small or big, promotes psychological well-being. Generosity is an act of kindness, whether it's a smile, a compliment, a gift, or something more substantial. Whenever we receive from others, we should feel and express gratitude. Those of us who live in the Western world are very fortunate to live in such safe times, have warmth, food, water, shelter, and the pleasures that come with it. We live better today than the Kings of the past did, with our luxury cars, centrally heated homes, designer clothing, and technical advancements. We are so very fortunate to be living in an age where we have had peace in our country. As long as we have good health, we have everything. Therefore, we should appreciate and express gratitude for these glorious riches every day. When we do, we further enhance our well-being. Many people look for reasons to complain instead of appreciating the good things we have.

As humans, we have an instinct to want more, right from birth, and without the ability to even speak or think, we ask for food by crying when we need it. As we grow older, we further learn to ask for the things we need. Still, then we start to want material things that we do not need because others have them or purely for the sake of wanting. Greed goes hand in hand with selfishness, and people do not like greedy, selfish people. So being greedy and selfish does come with a price. It causes struggle in relationships, working environments, friendships, and family life because they are not team players. Those living happy, balanced lives recognize and value the importance of being a team player within a unit.

Chapter 10

Family Awareness

Better Parenting

Anxiety-related issues are genetic, learned, and environmental.

If you suffer from anxiety-related problems, it is essential to break those patterns so that your children do not learn or develop similar anxieties. Your children are the parents of tomorrow. As such, the relationship you develop with them will play a massive part in your future happiness. They will become your friends, and if they have children, you will have Grandchildren, and on it goes. In all children you encounter, it is vital that you make a good impression or certainly not a bad one, as this may make a big difference to your life one day in the future. Those people who are dismissive of children overlook the importance of this.

Practice; Use a NURTURING style of parenting instead of a CRITICAL style.

Those who use a critical style of parenting use phrases such as;

Be careful you are going to fall and hurt yourself.

Look what you're doing -you're doing it wrong.

Give it to me, and I will do it properly; you are useless.

You will never be able to do that.

You are so clumsy.

Those that use a nurturing style of parenting use phrases such as;

You can do it; you're doing great, well done.

You can learn anything if you put your mind to it.

You are fine, get up, and try again.

Well done, you are improving so much.

Critical parenting styles cause children to doubt themselves and become insecure, whereas nurturing parenting styles teach children to become confident, assured, capable, and independent.

Make it be known to your children never to do anything that will disgrace themselves or their family. Help them to become family orientated and to develop loyalty and respect for others.

Teach them that everyone is born with a gift. Just because someone else is better at something doesn't mean that they are a better person.

Ensure they develop empathy, which is the ability to understand the feelings of others. An essential trait a child should learn. A child that learns understanding will grow up more balanced, happier, develop better relationships, friendships, and live a more stable life. You can do this by showing sensitivity towards others, nature, and animals.

Help them to understand that no one can have everything their way or get what they want when they want it. Spoilt children grow up with too much expectation and a lack of appreciation as adults. Spoiling children can make their adulthood very difficult.

Encourage creativity and imagination. All great things start with a dream; help them develop a "thinking outside the box" mentality by allowing them to dream.

Explain the importance of looking at situations as a WHOLE and not in PART. Just because something looks, sounds, feels, or tastes good doesn't mean it is good. Evaluating everything from all aspects will help make better, more informed decisions.

Encourage achievement with reward, but ensure that they have alongside plenty of emotional support and love. (otherwise, you risk creating a narcissist.)

Always allow your children freedom of speech, to articulate their feelings and share their experiences. Never punish them for this. Respect their honesty and encourage openness, so you can know who your children are. Many parents do not really get to know their children because they have forced them to behave and act in a way that stops them from being open and honest with them. This is because a child will behave in a certain way towards someone or an outcome they fear.

Demonstrate clear boundaries and rules before a situation occurs when possible, and explain what the consequences are. This way, they can only blame themselves when they break the rules, which will teach them responsibility and value.

Clearly define punishment, which is taking something away or giving something. All punishment must be fair to the incident and delivered instantly.

The Truth about Lying

We tell our children not to lie or be dishonest, often threatening to punish them if they do not comply. Yet, we teach our children to lie and be deceitful. Many parents (in Western world countries) tell their children that Santa Claus will be coming down the chimney with gifts at Christmas and that reindeers fly. We tell them that the tooth fairy will bring money in exchange for a tooth if left under the pillow. Parents encourage children to hide things; don't tell your Mum/Dad, make sure your sister doesn't find out, etc. There are many circumstances where this sort of thing occurs. But it's not all bad because there is a positive benefit when children lie and hide things. It develops their imagination and problem-solving ability. It also teaches them to understand that sometimes we have to keep our mouths shut. It's good to make children question their integrity.

As adults, lying has a positive aspect too. It is sometimes necessary for everyone to tell the occasional white lie to avoid a big drama, upset, or offend. And often, we are required to lie to protect. For example, if our partner or spouse said, do I look fat in this? To not offend, many would answer, "No, darling, you look great." In certain situations, a hospital doctor may have to tell someone injured in a severe car accident that the passenger was OK to protect them when it was actually a fatality.

There does come the point, however, when lying becomes unacceptable. When those white lies become fantasy lies used to impress others or deliberately intended to deceive - this crosses the line. This is where it becomes intolerable and highlights a lack of respect for others and a flawed moral compass. Sometimes it can mean that there is a much more significant mental health issue. Others who use fabrication in this way do get noticed, affecting how they are perceived. Credibility with others is vital for any type of success. Those that continuously lie do lose credibility from others and, as a result, are not trusted or taken seriously.

Entering into a Partnership

Whether it's business or personal, we should not entirely rely on our heart or gut feelings when committing to any long-term relationship. When we go all-in and enter into a relationship with someone or something, we are handing over our trust. And we hope that we have made the right decision because any long-term decision comes with an unknown element. Those that have experienced situations that have not worked out and suffered financial or personal struggles, often for many years, will know just how vital these decisions actually are. It happens every day. Although there is no way to avoid this entirely, we can significantly reduce the risk by being more aware of who or what we are dealing with. It is easy to become enamored by an image, a person's charm, or a level of success. Each person has many facets and will change according to each situation, whether it's work, home, formal, informal, or social. Most of us can put on a show for short periods when wanting others to think a certain way about us, but this does not always reveal who we really are under the surface. It takes time to get to know and understand how someone works. Suppose you decide to enter into any relationship or commitment that has long-term implications. In all cases, there is a need to look deeper into that situation to be confident that you are making the best decision. Your future well-being may depend on it. It's not about looking for fault; it's about being cautious and going in with your eyes open so that you have a good idea of what to expect if or when things get tough.

You hear people say they have fallen instantly in love, with a person, object, situation, or even a pet. Still, there is always a time when you can decide whether to retreat or go all-in. It doesn't matter how seductive something appears to be; there is still a moment of choice. As well as liking someone, you must also ensure that you are comfortable, feel safe, and that your values and goals are aligned with that other person or situation. If you need to, also ensure that you are protected legally. Withdrawing is never easy, but it is easier to withdraw and recover earlier than become stuck and suffer long-term. When you are dating someone you would like to be with long term, three ingredients will massively increase the odds of longevity. The first is attraction, as, without this, you have no foundation. The second is compatibility; otherwise, you may quarrel or frustrate each other too much. And the third thing is that you have common interests so that you can have endless fun together.

Top tip; Minimalize your risk by doing due diligence. As with all calculations, there are no guarantees, but limiting your risk for the long term is smart, and something that very few do. I am not saying to be a full-on detective searching for reasons not to go all-in. What I am saying is that we should be open-minded and not swayed by emotion alone. Any type of commitment needs to be a decision made with your head, not your heart.

Here are a few things to help you build a theme of the person you are dealing with. How does that person treat their children? If someone doesn't love their children do you think you have a chance long term? Listen to the reputation they have developed from those around them. How long have previous relationships lasted? What was the longest time they have stayed committed to someone or something? How have previous relationships ended? Were they acrimonious or amicable in a split? What is there relationship like with their parents? Look at the type of friends they have. Do they have ongoing issues related to the past? Have they have had help to deal with any problems? Ask what their main regrets in life are? Looking at these historical facts will give you some idea of what you can expect if things go wrong.

Financial Awareness

Financial worries and problems can make our lives miserable and cause us a lot of anxiety. We are not taught how to manage our finances at school, which I have always found surprising. It is one thing having no money but another to be in financial debt. Therefore, it is essential to keep on top of bills and financial associated paperwork. If you have a debt obligation, maintain communication with your creditors, and stick to financial arrangements or agreements.

Prioritize rent or mortgage payments so that no matter what, you have a roof over your head and do your best to protect your credit score.

Save for the things you want rather than putting it on credit or spending your money on things you do not need. Not only is this a better financial move but also a rewarding one where you will achieve a great deal of satisfaction in both the build-up and the receiving.

If you are fortunate enough to be in good financial shape, invest rather than save, and of course, help those less fortunate than you, whenever you can.

Quick reminder Guide

Use the hypnosis audios on a regular basis depending on your needs and situation.

Make sure you always validate beliefs with facts and evidence, not opinion or feeling. No proof – Its goof

Do not make exact plans too far ahead into the future. Focus on what you are doing in the now, looking ahead just 6 months forward. Any plans further into the future, keep loose and start working on the details of them when you get to the 6 months window.

Leave the past where it belongs – It's in the past for a reason, and it doesn't matter how much you want something back; it can never come back the same.

Accept situations immediately - Acceptance is the first step to recovery, speeds up any healing, and allows you to focus on solving the problem.

When things go wrong, know it will change because everything in life is temporary.

Don't allow someone else to spread misery onto you.

Know that you have to give to receive in this world.

Do not over expect in yourself or others as it is likely to lead to disappointment.

Live your life as sincerely and honestly as you can because a clear conscience brings a calmer mind.

Practice forgiveness- Holding anger will cause you to feel frustrated, aggressive, and miserable, so let go ASAP.

Life's flow is evolution and change, so be receptive to it and move with the times; otherwise, you will become stuck and left behind.

Remove negative people from your life. Toxic people will bring you down.

Forgive yourself as well as those that have hurt and upset you. Forgiving others doesn't mean re-establishing contact.

Don't regret anything that you have done. Just make sure you have learned from the experience and use that experience positively.

Don't take yourself too seriously; go easy on yourself and others. Being uptight is not mentally healthy for you nor those around you.

Meditate regularly as it cushions us in times of difficulty, develops our creativity, maturity, and rewards us with a calmer disposition.

If you have nothing good to say, don't say it unless it's for the purpose of constructive criticism, which should be delivered kindly.

Remember, we are all vibration - you get back what you put out.

Give freely to others less fortunate than yourself. (It doesn't have to be monetary)

Hello to the future, and Goodbye to the past

The gift of change is yours at last.

A life without purpose has no meaning or call

And a life without meaning has no purpose at all.

Create dreams and beliefs, in all that you do

Add action and passion, and make them come true.

Our journeys can be tough, and the challenges real

Use that new strength, to bounce over that hill.

Keep on with the journey, and never give up

That's how you earn the gift of luck.

One day be assured, the stars will align

And that is the moment for you to shine

All of the work, and all that you've learned

It's finally yours, so enjoy what you've earned.

Fulfilment in love, happiness, and health

And this my friends, is the meaning of wealth.

"Happiness is not something ready-made. It comes from your actions."

Dalai Lama.

www.ingramcontent.com/pod-product-compliance
Lightning Source LLC
LaVergne TN
LVHW010616100826
845148LV00014B/2992